Advance Praise For *Brave-ish*

"Niver's global travel exploits had me simultaneously chewing my fingernails and cheering her on as she challenged herself to greater and riskier feats in search of self. Compelling and engrossing. A must-read for fans of *Wild* and *Eat, Pray, Love!*"
— ALKA JOSHI, *New York Times* bestselling author of
The Henna Artist (Reese Witherspoon x Hello Sunshine Book Club Pick), *The Perfumist of Paris*, and *The Secret Keeper of Jaipur*

"Lisa Niver's *Brave-ish* is a page-turner and inspiration for anyone who finds themselves at rock bottom in mid-life. Through both grand adventures and small, life-savoring gestures, Niver pieces herself back together after heartbreak and hardship. Readers will have the great pleasure of traveling the world through Niver's stories and will be cheering her on. Don't miss this book full of heart, adventure, and, of course, courage!"
— CHRISTIE TATE, A *New York Times* Best Selling author
of *Group* and *BFF,* a Reese Witherspoon x Hello Sunshine Book Club Pick

Brave-ish

ONE BREAKUP, SIX CONTINENTS, AND FEELING FEARLESS AFTER FIFTY

LISA NIVER

Post Hill
PRESS

A POST HILL PRESS BOOK
ISBN: 978-1-63758-781-2
ISBN (eBook): 978-1-63758-782-9

Cover design by Conroy Accord

The author is represented by MacGregor Literary, Inc.

All people, locations, events, and situations are portrayed to the best of the author's memory. While all of the events described are true, many names and identifying details have been changed to protect the privacy of the people involved.

Post Hill Press
New York • Nashville
posthillpress.com

Published in the United States of America
2 3 4 5 6 7 8 9 10

*"Just when the caterpillar thought the world
was over, she became a butterfly."*

—CHUANG TZU

Thank you to my parents for their love,
support and for giving me both roots and wings.

TABLE OF CONTENTS

Broken Sky

I lay on the sidewalk looking up at the sky. Yesterday, I'd been mesmerized by Wat Rong Khun, a complex of white buildings made of glittering porcelain, better known as the White Temple. The temple was one of the main reasons we had traveled three hours and thirty minutes by bus from Chiang Mai in Northern Thailand to the smaller and less touristy Chiang Rai. I had walked across the long, glistening bridge over the calm lake to see the temple, which sat on what seemed to be an island, and could not believe how beautiful it was. Naga serpents slithered across the roof, intricate and stunning, so delicate they looked as though they had been made out of white lace and frosting.

I loved the mirrored reflections of the temple in the water and tried my best to capture them with my camera, but Fred chastised me for taking photo after photo of the same thing. *They're digital photos*, I thought, *why can't I take as many as I want?* As we walked around, I even managed to use a few Thai words, which I was trying to learn and speak as much as I could. My favorite phrase was *di mak mak*, which means "very good." I had used it when we bought our entrance tickets too, but Fred had been impatient with me talking to the man behind the counter, so we quickly moved on.

Now, however, I found myself lying on the ground trying to figure out what had happened. Fred stood over me, his eyes open too wide and his face getting redder and redder. Only a minute before, we had been discussing where to eat lunch. Chiang Rai, famous for its sacred religious sites and homestay visits for curious foreigners with local tribes, was also known for its cuisine.

We had wandered from our hotel along a wide street with proper sidewalks, and Fred walked single file behind me. Suddenly, without making a sound, like a stealth attack from behind, he grabbed hold of me and threw me down on the ground. As I lay there on the sidewalk, stunned and reeling from the impact, he reached down and took hold of my necklace. Made from a seashell, I cherished it and never took it off because it had been his first gift to me on an early trip to Fiji. He pulled on it hard, breaking the chain, and yanked it off me with such force that I feared it might have cut my neck.

I felt like I was being mugged in the New York City subway. But the man standing over me wasn't a mugger or a stranger—he was my husband, who was supposed to love me. He cast my necklace away from us as if the farther it went, the less I meant to him. He shouted, "You are a terrible person! You are disloyal! You are a terrible wife!"

I had slammed into the ground when he pushed me, and I might have been bleeding, or even had a broken arm or back, but I was too hurt and confused to care. I heaved myself up and tried to defend myself.

"I am a great wife!" I countered. "You always say that you love me so much and that I'm your favorite person! What is wrong with you? Why are you acting this way?"

Out of the corner of my eye, I saw a Thai man watching us nearby. Mortified, I thought, *Here we are in this spiritual place, a town that has more temples than hotels, and we are screaming at each other in the street.*

My next thought was, *What will happen to me if that man calls the police?* If the Thai police came, they would believe it was my fault. We were in a tiny town many miles and hours away from Bangkok or Chiang Mai, and I was a woman. The police would take my husband's side. Would I end up in Thai jail?

We'd been traveling in Southeast Asia for eighteen months, spending all day, every day, together on the road. Fred and I were seasoned travelers and this was our second big trip—on our first, an eleven-month trip after only a few months of dating, we got engaged. We had met online in 2007 when we were both working in Los Angeles, and immediately connected over our love of foreign lands.

That morning, we'd argued about our website, WeSaidGoTravel. com, which began after our first long trip together. Fred was angry that I had agreed to work on a video contest with our tech muse, Declan. The idea was to have travelers send in their favorite videos from around the globe and our judges would pick the best one. I was growing our YouTube channel slowly. The contest would help grow and promote the site, and I knew we needed more videos. While I loved the idea of a video contest, I knew I couldn't do it alone; there were already many challenges with the writing contests I was currently running on the website. Fred refused to work on the website and complained when I did. When Declan offered to help me, I accepted it like a drowning swimmer grabs a lifeline.

Fred had wanted to start a video contest in the past, but I'd always said no. We already had three writing contests a year that ended on Valentine's Day, the Fourth of July, and Thanksgiving that took up a huge amount of time and effort. I worried Fred's video contest would mean even more work for me, when he was already angry about me spending so much time on the website. Sometimes I even worked on my computer in the bathroom in our hotel room so he wouldn't be disturbed as I wrote blog posts, edited photos, and promoted our articles on social media in order to make money.

That morning, on a Skype video call with Declan, he broached a similar idea. After some discussion, I had said okay, so now Fred was angry. I had agreed to Declan's video contest, but not his. In Fred's mind, now I was disloyal and I liked Declan better. I wanted to be partners with Declan and be married to Declan. He was furious and hurled all these absurd accusations at me now as I stood opposite him on the sidewalk. I felt humiliated; I could not believe the stupid things he was screaming at me, loudly, in public.

I tried to steer the conversation back toward something remotely civil, to no avail. Finally, I took a deep breath and a step back. For a moment, both of us were silent. Then he turned and began walking away. I briefly considered following him. I thought maybe I could better explain why I had agreed with Declan, but something held me back. I always hated it when he got angry, but this time I felt he had gone too far. He had pushed me down. In broad daylight. When there were other people around. He was not drinking. And I knew that I had done nothing wrong.

Disoriented

I returned to our hotel room at Mantrini. Looking out to the patio, I felt like I was in a fishbowl. Could the people walking by tell that my marriage was broken? I felt nauseous. I could not stop crying or shaking. Was this the end? Could I forgive him again? Should I?

In my hand, I held the shell from my necklace. After Fred had stormed off, I managed to find it in the street. The clasp on the gold chain was broken, but I was glad that *it* had broken rather than my neck. I wasn't sure if I would ever fix it or wear it again. I took off my wedding ring and just kept staring at it. I knew I couldn't bring myself to put it back on.

I closed the shades and opened my computer to Skype with a friend. Carl was one of my best friends from college. I'd known him since my very first day at the University of Pennsylvania. When he answered in Los Gatos, California, I was crying hysterically.

"Take a deep breath. Are you okay? Are you safe?"

I told him I was in my hotel room in Chiang Rai, alone.

He asked me what happened.

"Oh God, Carl, he just went nuts. He pushed me onto the ground. He came up behind me, and all of a sudden, I was on the sidewalk and all I could see was the sky. He was shouting at me. People were staring. I can't believe this is happening."

Carl had met Fred multiple times and been an honored guest at our wedding. He had always known my boyfriends and protected me like a big brother. No one knew how bad things were between Fred and I—maybe even me; even so, Carl could hear that I was upset and quickly understood things must be terrible if I was calling him all the way from Asia, crying. Over the years, even when we had lived in different countries (Japan for him, Israel for me) we had always talked long distance, but usually to trade good news.

"Lisa," he said firmly, "there must be consequences."

Consequences? In that moment, I didn't understand what those consequences should be, mostly because I still felt that, on some level, I must be responsible for the situation. I had wanted to come to Asia, to get back on the road, because Fred was so unhappy in Los Angeles. I thought that if we were traveling, things would be better. But even halfway around the world, he was still unhappy. With no job or issues with the condo to complain about, he continued to whine, but now more and more frequently about me. Fred had always had gripes—my hair was turning gray or not perfectly straight—and once I had allowed a bottle of wine to fall out of his car when I opened the door, he called it "alcohol abuse." I hadn't realized that his unhappiness was the pattern.

I had been afraid that his video contest idea was a bad idea because I would be busier, and he hated that. But I really thought Declan could make it work. I had never imagined he would be so jealous, or that he would believe I was disloyal or liked Declan more. It didn't make any sense. I was grasping at straws and figured that if I was responsible, maybe I could also figure out how to fix it.

"What do you mean?" I asked.

Carl's first suggestion was that Fred should not stay with me that night. "Whenever he comes back," he said, "you need to tell him that he has to stay somewhere else."

"That doesn't sound very nice," I ventured, my voice full of hesitation. "He's my husband and I love him."

"What *he* did was not nice," Carl countered. "And if you were here in the U.S., he might actually be in jail. This is not about being nice. This is about what you need to do to take care of yourself and be safe."

I reluctantly said goodbye to Carl, shut down my laptop, and thought more about "consequences." This was not the first time Fred had been physical with me. Over the course of our relationship, particularly in the years since we had gotten married, Fred was frequently upset about my behavior, my appearance, even my being noisy. He complained about the lunches I packed him and that I ate my apples too loudly and held my sandwich with too many fingers. He hated when I talked on the phone to friends inside our house, so I'd taken to calling everyone I knew on my walk home from work. Earlier on our trip, he had stopped walking with me on beaches because my footsteps in the sand were too loud and would distract him. It upset him that I read too quickly on my Kindle and said that even when I switched pages noiselessly on the electronic device, it disturbed him. On a twenty-four-hour bus trip through India, he complained that I went to the bathroom too often. You could only go to the bathroom when the bus stopped, and sometimes it only stopped every six hours. Fred would not go every time we stopped, but I would. More and more, he used physical tactics to express his frustration. Sometimes, he pinched me when he got aggravated, which really hurt and left a bruise. The trip was not making things better. In fact, the longer we were away and the farther we traveled, the angrier he got.

I was on Skype talking to friends from Los Angeles who had moved to Beijing when Fred returned to our hotel room several hours later. They wanted me to come to China to be with them, but I wasn't ready to make any decisions about what to do. My shoulder and neck were still hurting from my fall, and while I had taken some Tylenol, I was in pain. My head throbbed. I wondered if I'd hit my head and perhaps had a concussion, but I also thought my headache might be due to confusion and emotional trauma from being harmed by my husband. I said a hasty goodbye to my friends and closed the computer.

Fred said, "Who were you on the phone with?"

"I was talking to Brent and Wendy," I told him. "I need my friends right now. We are so far away from home, and I feel really hurt and alone."

"Why are you telling everyone our business?" Fred demanded.

"Because I am devastated. Our marriage is broken. What you did is not okay. I have been sitting here in this hotel room, hysterical and upset. I cannot believe that you pushed me. You hurt me. You ripped my necklace. You made me *fall* in front of other people! And then you left."

"I was wandering the streets thinking about you," he said.

I looked at him, waiting for him to apologize. But he didn't. He never apologized. He always had an excuse.

"I thought you would follow me," he went on. "I kept looking back for you."

"I did think about following you. But what you did was wrong. You cannot push me." In truth, he had pushed me before. I had thought about leaving once and staying at my parents, but I was too embarrassed to admit what had happened, so I stayed at our condo.

But today he had crossed a line. He could have killed me. If I had hit my head on the concrete, he might have been calling my parents to tell them I was in the hospital in Thailand with a broken neck or dead.

He said, "I was upset that you agreed to do the contest with Declan."

As he spoke, something in me shifted. His feelings were hurt that I had taken the side of the tech person whom we paid to help me. Help that I desperately needed since he spent most of the day playing video games on his iPad while I worked tirelessly on the site.

"Our marriage is broken," I told him. "You cannot stay here tonight."

He was stunned. "Where am I going to stay?"

"I don't know, but you can't stay here."

He protested but I stood my ground. I knew he was waiting for me to change my mind. He seemed sad. But if he knew that he had acted badly, he was not taking responsibility.

Eventually, he agreed to leave and return to Chiang Mai, which was three hours away by bus. He would get a hotel room, and we would meet there in two days after I had time to think. I was crying, and before he left, he held me for a long time. My mind and my heart were at war. For months, we had been inseparable, but now he seemed like a stranger. How had this happened? I wanted so badly to ask him to stay and hold me all night, but I kept hearing Carl talk about "consequences." It was comforting to be held in the arms of my husband, and at the same time, my shoulder throbbed because this very person had thrown me to the ground.

He asked me if I was okay. I said I wasn't. Then he asked me again if he really had to go.

I took a deep breath and pulled away. "It's time for you to leave."

As I sat alone in my hotel room that first night, my mind raced through all of the bad or questionable decisions I had made over the course of our relationship. How could I have chosen to marry someone who would do this to me? What had I missed? Maybe, I reflected, I should have left him in Malaysia after he'd slapped me. Maybe, when he had stormed out of a salsa class on one of our early dates, frustrated because he was a beginner and I had more experience, I should never have gone out with him again. I was sure that somehow, some way, and even if it had only been by accident, I was responsible for his violent behavior and for putting myself in this situation.

As scenes from our marriage played in my head, I realized that from the very beginning, I might not have seen clearly who Fred was. Instead, I saw what I wanted him to be. I thought that he was my soulmate, the man I'd always wanted who would give me adventure and travel and make my dreams come true. But that was only a part of who he was.

I'd had trouble seeing my entire life, which led to a "clumsiness" that tended to end in accidents. As a child, I'd never been able to play sports because I couldn't see the ball coming at me. On the playground, I could never hit the tetherball, four square was difficult, and I was always picked last for any team. I'd almost drowned one year at summer camp during the swim test. I did know how to swim, but I jumped in and began swimming to the other side, and the water was cloudy so I couldn't spot the opposite edge of the pool. I just kept swimming and swimming, never getting anywhere. I think I was swimming at an angle toward the deeper end. The last thing I remember was sinking down toward the bottom. I couldn't keep going but I couldn't find the other side. One of the counselors jumped in and fished me out before I hit the bottom. For the rest of the summer, I sat on the steps of the pool while the other kids swam.

The sport I was forced to participate in throughout my childhood was skiing. My father had always loved skiing and we went on ski trips for every holiday break. Everything about skiing was a challenge. The skis and poles were heavy and I always felt like I was about to drop everything when we were walking to the mountain. Once we got to the top, I struggled to see a path down through the other skiers, making the process of getting down again overwhelming.

My childhood eye doctor admitted he couldn't correct my vision to 20/20 and sent me to a specialist who said that yes, while something was preventing me from seeing 20/20, it was nothing to worry about medically.

I had learned to compensate for the gaps in my vision by always working harder and trying harder than everyone else. I made straight As, sat in front of the classroom, and avoided tennis and tetherball because I just assumed I was lousy at sports. I never complained, so my parents didn't worry. Now I began to wonder, however, if there was some connection between my struggles with physical sight and my ability—or inability—to perceive people and situations accurately, as they really were. Maybe I was finally seeing the truth.

I barely slept that first night. The next day, I kept calling friends around the world as the time zones permitted. I spoke again to my friends in China who wanted me to get on a plane and come to them. I considered their offer, but since I could barely go five minutes without bursting into tears, I couldn't imagine going to the Chinese embassy in Bangkok to get a visa. Frankly, I couldn't imagine doing anything.

The following morning, I was exhausted but managed to get on the bus back to Chiang Mai. Fred typically did all of the paying and negotiating when we traveled, so it was the first time I had paid for anything in months. I did my best to talk to the driver in

Thai, but nothing felt *di mak mak*; instead, it felt like the universe had fallen out of place in the cosmos. Nothing made any sense.

I chose a seat by the window, which I thought might be more comforting and possibly make me feel less alone. I opened my Kindle but couldn't focus on the pages or remember what was happening in the story. As the streets of Chiang Rai drifted away behind me, I realized that I was going to have to travel much farther than this first leg back to Chiang Mai to find shelter and support.

When I got to Chiang Mai, I called Teresa, my best friend and college roommate. We'd had several calls over the past few days where she urged me to come home as soon as possible. That day, I was only aware of being on the phone with her for an hour or so. In reality, we spent more than four hours going round and round in the same conversation.

"If I buy you a ticket, will you get on the plane?" Teresa pressed.

"I'm leaving?" I asked. Two days had passed and the events unfolding still didn't make any sense. Why did she want me to leave Asia? I loved Asia. I loved traveling. I didn't feel ready to leave. Fred and I had been talking about finding a place to live for the next four months. I was happy to stay in Asia indefinitely, but I was tired of being constantly on the move. I wanted more stability. I wanted to settle into a neighborhood or town, to really work at learning the language, to make friends. We had talked about picking several places like Chiang Mai or Koh Samui in Thailand, Ubud in Indonesia, or maybe somewhere in Central America, closer to home, so we could visit on the way there or back, and staying in each one for four months. If I left now, how would I get here again without Fred? What if I never got back to Thailand?

"I can come to Thailand and fly home with you," she offered. "I'll fly from Philadelphia to Chiang Mai to pick you up."

"Why would you come to Thailand?"

"Are you going to get on the plane?" she continued. "Because if you are not going to get on the plane, I am coming to get you."

"Why am I leaving?" I was confused.

But Teresa was persistent, and by the end of the call, even I understood that I was not in any shape to stay in Thailand alone. I also knew I was not ready to see Fred. Leaving made the most sense for my safety.

Teresa offered to help me purchase the ticket, and I relented. But there was a problem. I had Fred's passport. I always carried both our passports and now I realized I couldn't leave Thailand without handing his off to him. Maybe I would have to see him, I said. After all, I couldn't abandon him in a foreign country without any means of getting home. Teresa suggested I leave his passport in an envelope at the front desk and email him after I was on the plane to tell him it was there.

My ticket booked, I hid in my hotel suite for the next forty-eight hours, eating cheese sandwiches for every meal while I Skyped with friends. People kept telling me that I was brave, that I was courageous. I actually looked up both words in the dictionary because I thought, perhaps, I had misunderstood their meaning. I was not brave; I was not courageous. The only thing I seemed capable of doing was crying and eating chocolate out of the mini fridge.

At one point, Teresa suggested I sit by the pool and read. So, I put on my bathing suit and went down and sat on a lounge chair beside the pool. However, I couldn't concentrate and I felt too exposed outside. I never even took off my robe. Instead, I pulled several towels over me and hid on my chair. I read for a few minutes before deciding I was going back inside to cry.

During all this, I still hadn't called my parents. I didn't want them to know what had happened because if Fred and I were somehow able to overcome this incident and put our marriage back together, they would never forgive him if they knew what had transpired. I recognized that they would, without any doubt, consider these events unforgivable, even if I did not. As it turned out, I found out later that they already knew—Fred had contacted them from Chiang Rai and said I was angry and not speaking to him, and that he had behaved badly. At the time, my parents didn't contact me about it; they waited for me to get in touch. Fred didn't mention the physical part of our encounter or hint that he might have harmed me in any way. He made it seem like a small marital spat.

My parents had been in intermittent contact with Fred during our trip because they were helping us with our condo, bills, and mail, and had power of attorney for both of us. His relationship with them had always been good. Fred and my mom often talked about their work with children in a school setting. My dad and Fred bonded over their love for me, and both wanted me to be happy.

I had promised Teresa that I would get on the plane, and I like to follow through on my promises. So, on the third day, I shoved all of my things back into the backpack that Fred had bought me for our trip and got ready to sneak to the airport. Fred had no reason to think I would actually be leaving Thailand. Even so, I crept downstairs and gave my key to the front desk along with an envelope that contained his passport and a note saying I was going home to the U.S. to think, that I needed time. I was concerned that if I saw him and heard his voice, I would cry, listen to excuses, and stay with him.

Yes, I had promised Teresa, but I had also promised Fred that I would love him and be married to him. I still wasn't sure if our marriage was over, but I had agreed to get on the plane. I didn't think about the fact that my condo was rented, I had quit my job, and I had been on foreign soil for more than a year and a half. I pushed all of these worries and objections aside and listened to the people I trusted.

Leaving the hotel, I felt scared, disoriented, and fragile, as though all my bones were going to break if I stepped the wrong way. Waiting for a *tuk-tuk*, a kind of open-air taxi, I reminded myself that I had made decisions in the past that also left me feeling like a derailed train. Years earlier, in my twenties, I dropped out of a top-five medical school to become an assistant preschool teacher, giving up the study of medicine and a lucrative career as a brain surgeon or gynecologist to play Simon Says and wipe noses. Later, after 9/11, I walked away from seven years of working on cruise ships and enjoying free travel to exotic locations to go back to teaching. Many times, people had told me I was ruining my life by opting for uncertainty over stability, but in reality, I had been opening the door to a much more exciting next chapter. As I left Le Meridien in Chiang Mai, I crossed my fingers that it would be true again. I only had to get in the *tuk-tuk* to the airport.

At last, one stopped, and I climbed inside with my backpack. As my *tuk-tuk* rounded the corner, I leaned against the frame of the open window, feeling the wind in my hair and watching the temples and the night market slip away in the distance. Memories of other travels flashed through my mind, and I recalled a tour guide I'd once had long ago when I spent a semester in Israel during college. My family had come to visit, and we'd been walking through the Old City while our tour guide Talia talked about language, and how the meanings of words have evolved over the millennia. She told us that the word "disoriented" stemmed from a time when the Orient, or Asia, was considered to be the center of the world. Therefore, when you got lost from your home or center, you were "disoriented." I kept thinking about this on the way to the airport, how "disoriented"—which meant spinning in circles, directionless, without a reference point or sense of true North—also meant literally having lost your Asia. I was losing my Asia now, along with my marriage, and my husband who had been my compass and the center of my map since we'd met seven years before. I thought I might never travel again. I thought I might never love again, or even smile or be happy again. Completely and utterly disoriented, I knew I had to get on the plane, but part of me still did not even know why.

Non-stop Flight to Crazytown

When I first returned to the United States from Thailand, I told my family and friends and anyone else who asked that I was back in America and living in Crazytown—where there was crying all the time. I cried standing in line at the grocery store. I cried in parking lots and on the side of the road in my car. I cried at home and on the beach. Everything made me cry: thinking of how mean Fred had been and how nice the people at the grocery store were being, and how I wasn't sure if I deserved to have new people be nice to me. I cried because I could finally go to dance class, which Fred had frowned on, but then I cried because I had missed dance. Things were a long way from *mai me ban ha* (which means "no problem" or "no worries" in Thai) and I definitely did not feel *di mak mak*. I missed Thailand. I missed my husband. I felt like I was going insane. My only hope was that someday I might graduate from Crazytown and move to Sucksville, where I hoped I would be free of this tremendous, never-ending crying.

In reality, I was living in my parents' house in Bel Air and feeling completely unsure about what to do next. I contemplated how I had ended up back in my childhood bedroom looking out the same window, with my sister's desk and the same mirrored closet doors. I wanted to be back in Asia. The days ticked by, and I struggled to know what to do with myself. I spoke on the phone with a few trusted friends repeatedly. I devoured books. I kept reading, hoping for answers. I read that you could not do a new thing in an old way, in order to find new ways, I took classes. I went to every exercise class and dance class I could find. I joined a gym that had a week of free classes and went several times a day. My friend's boyfriend joked that the gym was going to give me flowers to go away as I had cost them so much money. I tried kickboxing and pole dancing and hula hoop class on the beach and Israeli dance and anything I could find to keep busy.

I was still adding posts about my travels to the website and sending out newsletters, but I felt like a fraud. Was I still "We Said" if I was alone? I kept up with the writing contest and social media, and even though it felt robotic, I just kept going, like the Energizer bunny. Sometimes I wasn't sure if I could get from breakfast to lunch. I felt so lonely my skin was crawling. I was used to being next to Fred every single minute and it felt like I was missing a limb. One day, my goal was to go for twenty minutes without crying.

I also had reverse culture shock, which made it even harder to get my bearings. Even just navigating daily life in America was a challenge. One day I called Teresa to say I had found a dress for $29.95, but that seemed extremely expensive. Did she know how many nights I could stay in Thailand for $29.95?

"Buy the dress and we can discuss it when you get home."

Twenty minutes later, I called her from the gas station.

"Gas is very expensive."

She said, "Fill up the tank and we will discuss it when you get home."

I questioned all my decisions, and even the most basic outings left me feeling exhausted.

I owned the condo in Brentwood where Fred and I had been living before we left, but now it had a tenant with a one-year lease. I probably could have found a way to get the tenant to leave, but I wasn't sure I wanted to live in the condo anyway, with all the memories of Fred.

When I first arrived home, my sister flew to Los Angeles to support me. She and my mom persuaded me to go to my condo to retrieve some of my clothes from a locked closet. When I unlocked the closet door and touched all of Fred's clothes, I felt close to him again. When we got back to my parent's house, my sister asked, "Don't you feel better now? You have your things."

I burst into tears as I sat on the floor among the boxes. "I don't care about these things. I miss my husband."

Back in Los Angeles, I reflected that this was not the first time I had been at a crossroads and returned to my parents' house. In my early thirties, I moved in with them after 9/11 when my travel company went bankrupt. I went back to teaching, found an apartment, moved out, and put a new life together, piece by piece. But this time, after nearly two years of roaming around Asia, I felt like I had cut too many ties. I had quit my job and sold my car before we left, and being married to Fred had loosened my connections with friends. It seemed that my friendships were always causing problems. If I had friends over for dinner, he complained about the money spent on food. If I was on the phone with Teresa, he complained that he needed quiet. Even when we were abroad, he complained I spent too much money in internet cafés writing to friends. I wanted him to be happy, so I'd stopped devoting as much time to these friendships. Now I had never felt more alone. Could I weave my life back together? It all seemed daunting and impossible.

Growing up, I had always wanted to go away, to break away from the familiar, but I was always scared to leave. Once I arrived in a new place, I was happy, but there were often tears while getting ready. I never knew what to take with me or how to make it fit into a bag. And for the last few years, Fred had always been alongside me.

In high school, I went to all the proms and school dances, but usually with a family friend. I still hadn't really kissed a boy. I felt like there was a secret teenage code I didn't understand. Once when I was at a party in LA, a boy asked me, "Do you want to go on a walk? It's hot in here." I thought, *It is hot in here. Yes, let's go outside!* I was surprised when he wanted to kiss me. I didn't even like him; I had only agreed it was hot. How was I supposed to know when "go on a walk" actually meant go on a walk and when it meant, "Do you want to kiss me?" Had I missed a class in code words?

Now back in my childhood bedroom, I worried that, decades later, I still didn't understand relationships. Was what happened with Fred my fault? Had I missed the signals or misunderstood the code? I made up for being dorky in high school by dating several someones seriously in college and with many other relationships during my time on the high seas. I thought I knew what I wanted, and when I first met Fred, I felt connected to him, certain he was the one. Maybe I had only been naïve once again.

If I'd tried harder, been better, kept going despite the odds, would things have worked out differently?

I called my friend Brooke and told her, "I am a failure. Fred is right. I am a bad wife."

"The only failure," she assured me, "would have been if you'd stayed with him. You have to take care of yourself and be safe."

"But I promised him for better and for worse, for richer and for poorer, in sickness and in health, '*til death do us part*.'"

"Even if you promised 'til death do us part," she countered, "you did not promise to stay until he killed you."

That was sobering. There was no denying Fred's violence had been escalating, and even though I'd always known he had some issues, I had felt like we were working together to be the best people we could be. Now it seemed like maybe I had been working hard to help him grow while he'd been working to hold me down.

I went to see Rabbi Eli Herscher at Stephen Wise Temple, the same temple where I celebrated my bat mitzvah many years earlier. I knew I needed help to figure out my next steps, and he had been counseling people in troubled marriages for decades. I had missed participating in my Jewish community while I was traveling and had been going to Shabbat services every Friday, even though I cried through many of them.

Rabbi Herscher told me numerous things over the course of many meetings, but two of his insights really struck me.

"First of all," he said, "in a Jewish wedding, we do not say 'til death do us part.'" The second was, "We do not push strangers in the street."

I thought hard about that one. We don't even push strangers. And yet, my husband had pushed me. Yes, I had declared our marriage broken, but the reality was that Fred and I were still married, even if separated by a giant ocean. I needed a next step, but I wasn't sure what it should be.

"I know you, and I know how you think," my friend Willow told me. "This is not a problem that's going to be solved by Monday. This is not a figure-it-out-over-the-weekend type of situation. We need to make a plan for you, but I'm talking about a plan for today, maybe for the weekend, or maybe for the next two weeks. Everything is not going to be fixed right away. It's going to take a lot of time. It took time to get into it, and it will take time and effort for you to get out of it. You can do it, but at the end of the day, the first step is deciding what you want and how you want to be treated."

I knew she was right. An optimistic part of me deep down hoped that somehow a solution would appear, miraculously making everything all better. But another part of me realized that getting things back to the way they were was impossible.

CHAPTER 3

Baby Steps

I'd torn apart my life before when it wasn't working out and managed to build it back into something new. When I arrived as a freshman at the University of Pennsylvania in 1985, I was pre-med and convinced that I was on my way to becoming a doctor. I had chosen to go to Penn to try out life on the East Coast where my parents had grown up.

In those first days, I met Teresa, who became my best friend in college. When there were things I didn't understand, I would call Teresa for help, like when I was getting ready for class. I'd worn a uniform for six years in high school and didn't have any fashion sense. "Teresa, I really need your help," I would say, calling her on the phone from upstairs.

"Lisa, if I've told you once, I've told you a thousand times," she replied. "Everything goes with jeans."

How could everything go with jeans? They were *blue*. But I trusted Teresa, so I listened anyway.

I continued my studies of Hebrew for my language requirement and went to services on Friday night at the campus Hillel.

My sophomore year, I dated Nathan, whom I'd met in my chemistry class. He was one year older, smart, handsome, and he was Jewish. He seemed to check all the boxes. He took me out to expensive dinners and bought me fancy green and blue sweaters from Benetton. Sometimes it felt like playing grownup because other people were having dates with pizza on paper plates and we went to some of the finest restaurants in Philadelphia. Nathan was the first man I ever saw naked and the first person I ever had sex with.

I thought I loved him, but as the year went on, he became increasingly demanding and controlling. He hated anything that took time away from him, and he was particularly jealous of my friendship with Teresa.

I was also making plans to spend a semester abroad in Jerusalem, which I had wanted to do ever since I fell in love with traveling on a family trip to Israel in high school. Nathan tried to change my plans. He said that if I was away for the second semester of my junior year, I would miss his graduation and that I should wait until after he graduated and then go—but that was not my plan. I wanted to go during my junior year, and I had to be at Penn for my senior year in order to apply to medical school. He was angry and we fought about it repeatedly. I refused to change my plans. I was adamant about going to Israel and we broke up.

On the night before the MCAT, Teresa and I had done laundry and I had gone to bed early so I could get up early to take the test. That year, Teresa and I had singles in Ware College House, and for some reason, my socks were drying on a rack in her room. I had all of my clothes laid out for the morning, except for socks.

Sometime around midnight, I woke up to someone pounding on my door. It was Nathan, and he wanted me to stay at his house that night. I had been missing him, even though I knew we could not be together. I knocked on Teresa's door to get my socks.

When Teresa opened the door and saw Nathan, she was immediately prepared for battle. I didn't think that he'd come over to intentionally sabotage my MCAT results, but Teresa did. She was adamant that this was never going to happen. She said, "I will not give you your socks. You need to rest before your test. Go back to sleep and tell him that you will see him afterward." She closed the door. Discussion over. I told Nathan that I couldn't go because I had no socks, and he left. I never saw him again after that incident. Thank goodness for Teresa. I was done with him and I did well on the MCAT.

I left for Israel at the start of second semester in my junior year. I took classes at Hebrew University's Rothberg International School and lived in a dorm in the Mount Scopus section of the city. Every week we took a field trip to interesting historical locations around the city. As the weeks went by, I even met a lovely boy from Islip, New York, who became my boyfriend.

I learned a lot that year about how life looks different from the other side of the street, or of a country, or the world. It all made me wonder, where would I live? What did I want to do? Did I really want to study medicine? What people and things and ideas were really important to me? Being away I had encountered new vistas and new ways of thinking. I wanted to soak up more places. With all of the many choices before me, which ones would I choose?

During our senior year at Penn, Teresa and I shared an apartment in one of the high-rise dorms with two other girls. Most nights, I left the library around 9:00 p.m. and walked to the gym to pick up Teresa. She and another one of our roommates, Elizabeth, both worked as lifeguards at the gymnasium pool and were often on duty at the same time. One day when I picked her up, I commented, "I come to the gym every day but I never work out or even go inside."

"What would you want to do at the gym?" Teresa asked.

I thought for a minute, then said, "Well, I'd like to swim but I'm afraid that I am going to drown again."

Teresa had been teaching swimming for years and was in love with the idea of helping me learn to swim again. "Just try to drown with both Elizabeth and I watching you like hawks," she said. "I promise you will be okay."

"But I can't swim in the big, fancy, Olympic-sized pool with all the other students," I protested. "They are all really good and I will barely be able to swim one lap."

"Swim one lap," Teresa countered. "Get in the pool, push off at the end and say 'one hundred!' as if you've just done one hundred laps. Then you won't have to feel wimpy at all and everyone around you will be jealous that you swam so much."

Finally, I agreed, but I was wary. I was still worried about being embarrassed, and I was not convinced that the other people around me would not think it strange that I was a beginner at age twenty. But Teresa believed in me and wanted to help. And I really, really wanted to not be afraid of the water.

The first time we went to the pool, everything felt challenging. I got lost in the locker room. I didn't have a lock. I put my fingers through my swim cap. I was ready to give up and I hadn't even touched the water, but Teresa shared her locker with me and gave me another cap.

I did not swim for very long on that first day. I clung to the side of the pool and Teresa encouraged me to try a few strokes. She promised it would get easier.

The next time we met, I knew where to go. I had my own cap and lock, and just being at the pool did not feel as bad. Teresa handed me a workout list of strokes and laps, but I handed it right back. "Just teach me one part at a time," I told her. Under her guidance, I did drills with arms or legs only. In those first sessions, it felt like we swam for hours, but in reality, it was probably only thirty or forty-five minutes. As the days went on, I worked on my breathing. Then I began to work on crawl and backstroke. I even began to kind of like swimming. I realized that with the right teacher, I could probably do anything. Maybe I would never swim like Teresa and look like a mermaid, but now I did not look like a drowning minnow either.

Penn was very pre-professional, and that year it seemed like everyone around me was applying to graduate school. My boyfriend was applying to law school, I was applying to medical school, and most of the Wharton students had already lined up jobs at major firms on Wall Street. Even Teresa, an English major, had landed a high-paying job at Anderson Consulting. I was nervous about my applications and trying to decide where I should apply. I fretted that I would not get in anywhere, but when I started to work on my applications, I realized how much I had accomplished in my four years at Penn. I had strong grades, high MCAT scores, and several teacher references, including one from my independent study research advisor.

Ultimately, I was accepted to all the medical schools I applied to, including UCSF Medical School, one of the best medical schools in the country. After four years of East Coast weather, I was ready to return to California. My boyfriend had gotten into Stanford Law School, and almost all of my other friends, including Teresa, were setting off to new jobs and cities after graduation.

On my first day at UCSF, we had a lecture by a professor of psychiatry who welcomed us to the school and began talking about what our journey would be like over the next four years as medical students. He said, "Look to the left of you. Now look to the right of you..." I thought to myself, *I know this speech, he's going to say that only one of us is going to make it.* But that was not what he said next. Instead, he said, "At least two of you, if not all three of you, think that it is a mistake that you are here. This is called 'imposter syndrome.' You are worried that you are not good enough, that you are not prepared enough, that you won't make it. We will do everything in our power to help you succeed and become doctors, but you have to do the work on the inside and believe in yourself. We picked you. We believe in you. We want you to graduate. If you need support, ask for it. Do not be afraid to get help."

His talk touched a nerve. I was definitely nervous about starting medical school, but I was proud to be at UCSF and I wanted things to go well. Before I'd officially accepted, I'd spoken to at least ten doctors who were family friends, and nearly all of them tried to dissuade me from pursuing a career in medicine. But I wanted to help people. I got in. I knew there would be challenges, but I crossed my fingers and steeled myself to work harder than I ever had before.

Every day when I walked to school, I passed a group of children playing in the yard of the UCSF Children's Center, which was directly across from the entrance to the medical school. With my heavy load of books and four hours of lectures and three hours of lab ahead of me, I just wanted to play outside with those kids. Finally, one day in December, I went inside and spoke to the director and asked if I could come in and volunteer. She said that if I had time with all my classes, I was welcome. When I thought more about it afterwards, I realized that I truly did not have time, but it got me thinking. I began to wonder if I was in the right place after all.

That year, I lived with my friend Christy, another UCSF med student, in an apartment near Golden Gate Park. And one day, as

I wandered by the carousel, I realized there was an art class taking place in a building in the park. When I walked inside, I saw people of all ages and descriptions working with clay on pottery wheels. At Penn, I had taken an art class with live nude models and we sculpted them in clay. Now, watching the group before me shaping their pots, I remembered how much I'd loved that class and thought, *Maybe I need more clay in my life.* Maybe I needed more new places and activities, and as my art teacher always said, "Walk across the room and change your perspective."

Over winter break, I began to think that medical school was not my best choice. It was strange; I had been on this track for many years and now that I was here, it seemed odd that I might not want to be a doctor after all—but I felt very calm about it. I could feel in my bones that I might need to find another path.

Back at school, I went to see the dean and shared my concerns. She said, "Lisa, you are so young. I would love for you to take a year and find yourself and make sure that this is the right path for you. However, since you are a first year, the Dean of Admissions will need to decide whether to grant you a one-year leave or not. You will also need to speak with our school psychiatrist."

I not only had to meet with the psychiatrist, but also with the same doctors who had interviewed me when I applied. Rather than try to help me, however, they wanted to ascertain what they had done wrong in selecting me. How could they more effectively pick students who would not want to drop out? They kept asking me if I felt unprepared because I was a liberal arts major, but I had a science minor from Penn, and I did feel prepared. The work was hard, but I had managed, even though the labs in particular were very challenging. Frankly, I thought they needed more liberal arts students like me so students would think more about their patients as people and not just about what science could do.

The school psychiatrist was a lovely woman who was genuinely concerned about me. She told me that whatever I decided, she hoped that someday, if I did not return, I would be able to simply say, "It was not the path for me." I had long planned to go to medical school and here I was, but was it the best place for me to grow for the next four years? I still loved science, but did I want to spend my entire twenties inside that building and in training? Even summer vacations would be taken up by studying for the boards or interviewing for residency programs. I was conflicted about not being in school, but I was also curious about what might happen next if I decided not to return. In the end, I spoke to the Dean of Admissions, and he granted me a one-year leave. Around this time, my college boyfriend broke up with me. We had tried to keep seeing each other since we were both living in the Bay Area, but our packed schedules had made it challenging and we saw each other less and less.

I started to volunteer at the UCSF Children's Center and was quickly offered a part-time job as a preschool teacher's assistant. I was thrilled to be outside on their playground every day, singing with the children and blowing bubbles. Every day was different, and they let me create lessons that focused on science and math. I also took a job at Planned Parenthood, along with two other part-time jobs to make rent. I went to my different jobs and tried to determine what I should do next. I was busy, and I loved my time at the Children's Center, but I didn't exactly feel challenged. I missed my boyfriend, and although I went on a few dates, I wasn't interested in something casual. Working at Planned Parenthood in 1990, I was well aware of the risks of contracting HIV. Everything felt up in the air.

Twenty-five years after leaving medical school, I sat in my child-hood bedroom once again, trying to decide what to do with my life—all my thoughts about education and career plans, med school and teaching, and personal relationships in flux in my head. I needed to decide what I wanted to happen with my marriage. I had to earn money. I had to figure out what to do about the web-site and whether or not I should keep writing. Everything, especially the website, reminded me of Fred.

CHAPTER 4

Diving Deeper

After leaving medical school, I was looking for adventures, and since I had overcome my fear of water and learned how to swim, maybe, I thought, I could learn to scuba dive. I figured that if I had overcome my fear of the pool, the ocean might be the next step.

I signed up for a six-week scuba course that met once a week. I was both terrified and excited. The instructor was highly experienced and talked about his exotic dives around the world. We started out by practicing in a pool, and I was terrible, easily the worst student in the class. I tried hard to listen to the instructions, and figure out how to connect the different hoses and pieces of important safety equipment, but the multiple steps of attaching and detaching and breathing and not breathing left me confused. I'd always had issues with left and right, and the instructor kept talking about the "right-hand release" for the weight belt, or how to set up the regulator with the gauges on the left side. I was slower than everyone else because I was thinking, *Which is my right hand? Does this valve open to the right? Did I just use my left hand?* Eventually I developed my own ways to remember how everything fit together.

I learned to set up the tank and the Buoyancy Compensator Device (BCD), which is a vest that fills with air and lifts you up to the surface from underwater, and I practiced using the regulator that was attached to the tank so that I could breathe.

The hardest exercises for me involved practicing for emergencies and sharing air. In the event that your regulator malfunctions or you are low on air, you can share air with a buddy. In reality, every tank has two regulators, and it would be possible for two divers to be on the same tank at the same time, but in this exercise, we had to share a single regulator. I hated this exercise and every time I gave away my regulator, I bolted to the surface. I practiced with several different partners and even the instructor himself, but I still could not do it—until, after the instructor patiently explained the process for the umpteenth time, I realized that I hadn't understood the instructions correctly. I had been focused on "give your regulator away" but it turns out that there was another step first. First, take a breath! Second, give your regulator to the other person. I was already out of air when I shared my regulator, which meant I'd had no choice but to surface. I had been missing the most important step of taking care of myself first.

When we went to the beach in Monterey Bay for our first ocean dive, we had an extra instructor. For the cold water diving, we had thick wetsuits and needed more weight to compensate for the air trapped in the suits. We had to carry our tanks and gear and weights from the parking lot through the sand, and it felt like walking through molasses.

We did our surface checks and buddy checks, and then we descended. It was magical to go from being on the surface with the sea otters to being underwater in a kelp forest. During the drills, I did everything perfectly. From the mask removal to the simulated out-of-air exercise, I was calm and collected, waited my turn, completed the drills, and nearly enjoyed every second. After we surfaced, our instructor complimented me on successfully sharing my air and asked me what was different this time. I said, "Well, I never almost drowned in an ocean. I guess I feel more comfortable." He then confessed that he had brought along the extra instructor for me because he'd anticipated that I'd need one-on-one assistance.

The course had a few more ocean dives after that, and despite the cold and the heavy gear and many missteps, I walked away from the class loving scuba. I was proud that I'd learned to do something new—in the ocean, no less—but now how could I keep diving? I had chosen one of the most expensive sports with the most expensive gear. I had picked a sport where I needed a watch computer to make sure that my ascent was safe—and that was just the beginning. Most of the best diving locations, I learned, were exotic and far from California, requiring flights, hotels, and more training. It was hard to see how I could make scuba a regular part of my life due to the cost, but I liked it enough that I knew I wanted to figure it out.

Now, after Asia, I felt the same. I needed to figure it out.

While sitting at my parents' place, stewing in extreme self-doubt, I called my friend Richard Bangs for advice. Richard is known as the father of adventure travel, renowned for his river rafting first descents around the world. We had met at a travel event in Los Angeles a few years back and he had always been helpful. I wanted his thoughts on whether I should continue We Said Go Travel, and if he thought I could make it as a travel writer. He mentioned that he was filming an Orbitz web series in Puerto Rico and they wanted a segment on LGBTQ travel. He asked, "Lisa, if we invited you to join us in Puerto Rico and you were in charge of the segment, who would be your first call?"

Without a second's hesitation, I answered, "I would call Dean Nelson who co-created the Mr. Gay World competition. He could tell me if there is a Mr. Gay World Puerto Rico, and if there isn't, he could probably put me in touch with someone interesting."

Richard loved that answer and invited me to be the co-host of the series. It was huge. I would be the co-host of a bona fide series on a major travel platform, working with real professionals. I had been growing the YouTube channel for We Said Go Travel, but for those segments I had to do everything myself—find the locations, research the story, charge the batteries, make all the calls, film, edit, and host. My dream was to work with a team who would share some of these responsibilities. I accepted immediately and booked a plane ticket to Puerto Rico.

A few days before I was set to leave, my phone rang. It was Fred.

I panicked. Did I even want to talk to him? Finally, I picked it up on the fourth ring.

"I bought a plane ticket to come see you in Los Angeles," he said. "I'll be there on Monday."

"I will not be in Los Angeles on Monday. I'm filming a segment for Orbitz in Puerto Rico."

Fred got upset. "I bought a plane ticket to come see you! I am trying to save our marriage."

"Fred, you bought a ticket without even speaking to me," I said. "We haven't talked in weeks, and you picked what worked for you without even asking me if it was okay. Just because you want to come here doesn't mean that I am sitting at home, holding my breath, waiting for you to finally want to talk."

"I haven't called you because you asked me not to," Fred fired back.

I acknowledged that this was true but reiterated that calling me out of the blue and announcing a visit was not the right way to reconnect. He told me he'd read a book on anger issues and relationships and thought we could go to counseling together. His plan was that I would "keep track" of his behavior.

"So, you want me to be your kindergarten teacher and grade you on your behavior and keep track of whether you are improving?"

At last, he fumed, "Fine. I won't come visit. But I booked the flight on our joint credit card, you will either have to cancel it or pay for it." And he hung up.

I begrudgingly called the airline on his behalf. Suddenly, I was very glad that I had plans that did not involve him at all.

The plan was to be in Puerto Rico for six days, and we had a packed shooting schedule. During the day, my confidence stayed with me. I was on camera and being a professional. But every night in my hotel room, I cried. I was alone. I was confused. I was unsure about whether I had made the right decision coming here. What might have happened if Fred and I had met in Los Angeles? Could we have worked things out? Then I woke up one morning and felt suddenly better. I felt a glimmer of clarity. I was angry with Fred for intruding on my trip. I decided that for this film shoot, I was going to be Lisa Niver—not Lisa Niver Kozel.

When I met up with Richard, I told him about the change, and he filmed a video intro of me as Lisa Niver. Didrik, the cameraman, said, "Wait, that's not her name."

Richard looked directly at him, and I felt his answer in all of my cells as he said, "She can have whatever name she picks, and she picks Lisa Niver." I took a deep breath and knew that there would be many more steps, but this was a good one.

Over the next few days, we visited Ponce and Fajardo, and I met Mr. Gay World Puerto Rico, who took me dancing at a night-club on Saturday night in Santurce. I hoped to find time to go scuba diving. As Fred was always against it when we traveled—he thought it was too expensive—I hadn't been in a long time and scuba was not a part of the original itinerary.

Then one afternoon, Didrik came up to me and said, "I am really sorry, but I have some bad news. I hope you can work with me on this." I was prepared for him to say that they were shutting down filming, that Orbitz had backed out of the series, that they needed to replace me as a co-host and go in a different direction.

Cautiously, I replied, "Okay...."

"Tomorrow," he said, "I need you to get up very early and go scuba diving."

I gave him a giant hug with a very real smile across my face. I was beaming. *I'm going scuba diving*, I thought, *and I am away without Fred! People like me and want to work with me. They made this happen for me. I can do this.*

The next day, I dove at Copamarina Resort on the south side of the island along The Wall, a cliff of coral some twenty-two miles long that drops down to a depth of over 1,500 feet. I felt strong and happy. The day after, I filmed alone with my own cameraman at the healing waters of Aguas de Coamo, the legendary Fountain of Youth, which locals claim were discovered by Ponce de Leon. I met a local TV correspondent, Ramon, and he agreed to be in my segment while I hula hooped near the waters. I was willing to try anything—talk to strangers and reporters, film in my bikini while hula hooping. Things were changing.

On our last day, Richard and Didrik and I went to Toro Verde National Adventure Park, home of the second longest and highest zipline in the world, called "The Beast." I had only ever been on a zipline once before—a very tame, family-friendly zipline in Palau. I was scared. More than that, I freaked out. On the schedule it said "zipline," and the entire day I hoped that we would run out of time, or that it would break, or that our car would break down, or something would happen so that I didn't have to tell anyone I was too scared to go on this zipline. After we arrived, they put a microphone on me and started to get everything ready, and I was terrified. I forgot to speak Spanish to the man putting on my harness. I started asking him in English, "Are you sure this is a good idea? Would you let your grandmother do this?" He didn't understand me, but fortunately, this was all hilarious on camera. Didrik loved it and told me that I should say that line every time.

The operator pushed us off and I began screaming my head off. We went whizzing through the air and, at first, I was terrified, but then I realized, it is beautiful in the rainforest. I was floating above the trees. It was green and lovely, and I flew through the air like a bird! I realized I loved this ride, and then I screamed because I was happy! At the end of the line, I heard myself ask, "Can we go again? That was GREAT!"

The rest of the trip went smoothly, and at the end, both Richard and Didrik told me how much I improved every day. They said I was a natural. And for the first time, I thought, *thank goodness I came back to America*. Maybe I had finally left Crazytown for Sucksville, or maybe this town had another name like Have Job or Will Travel or Start Fresh. Maybe I would actually be okay.

On the Slopes

When I returned from Puerto Rico, I met with a divorce attorney a friend recommended. Maybe I would get back the life I had before I met Fred, or maybe my new life would even be better.

But then—the questions. I had warned Margot, the attorney, that I might cry in her office. I had warned her that I did not *want* to cry, but I might—and that if I did, I still wanted her to help me as a lawyer. I already had a therapist, I needed someone to help me focus on the legal issues. After my trip to Puerto Rico, I knew I could not go back to a life with Fred. I wanted to keep traveling, but not with him. I wanted my name back and I wanted to move on, even if that meant deciding our marriage was over.

I had to answer endless questions about how we had left things and the state of our business. The answers to all of these questions were complex.

"Who owns the business?" she asked me.

"Well, Fred came up with the name," I said, "but I do all the work."

"But what does the paperwork say?"

"What paperwork?" I asked. "It's digital. There is no paperwork."

"How do you pay taxes?"

"I just pay whatever my accountant tells me to."

Margot wanted to know if we had an LLC or board papers or any other documentation. We did not.

I felt foolish for not taking steps to make our business and our shared interests in it official. I offered to start creating the paperwork immediately, but Margot cut me off. "Don't get any papers now," she told me. "In fact, it might not even be a good time for you to be working on the website at all." She explained that if the website was a business that belonged to us both, and I grew it while we were legally separated, I would potentially owe him more money if I had to buy my half of the business back. I was stunned. Not work on the website? How could I be a travel writer without my blog? After all the hours I had devoted to writing articles and mastering WordPress, going to networking events, and learning to edit in iMovie, I couldn't imagine just turning away from it all. If I couldn't work on my website, I had to find other outlets I could write for. I began to run through all of my connections and brainstorm.

While Fred and I were traveling, a friend had started to write for the *Huffington Post*. I imagined the travel editor received many pitches, and wondered in what other section my stories might fit. I sent a pitch to *HuffPost* 50 about my forty-fifth birthday in Bagan where I'd had a disastrous bicycle experience—I called it "5 Years Until I am 50"—which they accepted. Now that I was home, I noticed another travel writer had posted an article link to *USA Today* 10Best, which had a section at the bottom with the headline "Write for Us." I was astonished to see that one of the cities they needed a 10Best expert for was Los Angeles. I had only been back in LA for what felt like thirty seconds, but I figured I had grown up here and they didn't need to know how long I had been away.

I reached out with links from my recent clips, and they emailed back: "Welcome to *USA Today* 10Best!"

The first story they assigned me was "10 Best Places for Lunch in Los Angeles." LA is an enormous city, so I decided to focus on places to eat on Ventura Boulevard in the San Fernando Valley, which was near my house. I included personal family favorites, such as Bamboo Chinese Restaurant and Mogo's Mongolian BBQ, where I'd eaten since I was a little girl, threw in a few new restaurants, and called it "Los Angeles Lunching: A Variety of Savory Venues on Ventura Boulevard in the Valley" and hoped they liked alliteration. They did, and shortly after it was published, a local PR firm called me to pitch a story on Tee's on the Green, a new burger place in Tujunga. A week later, they invited me to a restaurant opening at The Nice Guy. With every story that went live, more PR teams reached out to pitch pieces on local bars and eateries, and I realized that I would be invited anywhere if I told people I'd write about them in *USA Today*. This was good, as going out was helpful for my morale—it got me out of my parents' house, and if a friend joined me (because the PR people usually offered a plus one), I might spend as much as an hour or more not thinking about Fred or my divorce.

My friends told me I was taking steps and making progress. But when I wasn't going to restaurant openings, the days still dragged. Being in the same city day after day—one where I already knew how to speak the language—meant I had a lot more time on my hands than I was used to having. In between edgy new cuisines and craft cocktails, I kept going to therapy and working on my resume and trying to envision a future without Fred.

I missed going to Shabbat services on Friday nights and reflected that I had loved being a part of the Hillel at Penn as much as I'd loved Jewish summer camp. Twenty years earlier, when I had put a pause on medical school, I'd felt a similar sense of drift and uncertainty. I'd known I needed new goals and ambitions to ground me, but I didn't know what they should be. At that point, I had tried out many different services and loved Sha'ar Zahav, which was located in the Mission District. The weekly healing service gave me room to ponder all my questions, and I was hopeful that my centuries-old religion could help me have faith, find answers, and feel confident in my choices. Eventually, Rabbi Flam helped me create my own healing *mikveh*, a sacred Jewish ritual of purification done in water, which helped me close the chapter on Penn and med school.

Once I left medical school, it became clear that the salary from my work as an aide at the children's center and my other part-time jobs just wasn't cutting it. I began taking classes at San Francisco State University to earn enough credits to become a full-fledged teacher. SFSU had a renowned education department, and after trying out a few extension classes, I found myself in the Master's program. Through a connection I'd made while volunteering at city hall, I applied for a part-time job at Pacific Primary, a private preschool that paid me enough so I could quit all my other jobs and focus on my degree. I ultimately earned my Master's and received an award from SFSU for being a distinguished graduate student.

When I finished my degree, I was offered a raise at Pacific Primary, but it was for my same part-time, afternoon assistant teacher position. I wanted to stay but I needed more hours. I found a new job working as lead teacher at two sites for the San Francisco Unified School District, which meant that between the two part-time positions, I now had roughly three-fourths of a full-time job. It was an improvement in title, money, and status, but after a year, I was abruptly told in a staff meeting that one of the SFUSD schools was suddenly closing. It meant that I had only one-half of three-fourths of a full-time job.

When my friend Willow heard what happened with the school closing, she suggested to me half-jokingly, half-seriously, "What about working at Club Med?" She had just taken her young daughter there on vacation, and she told me, "Those GOs who ran the activities sure looked like they were having a great time. If I were single, I would pack my bags and go work on the beach with them. They would hire you in two seconds for the children's department." I trusted her implicitly. I thought, *Maybe I should consider it.*

As the weeks went by, I thought about what she said. What if I did work with kids at the beach instead of a classroom? What if someone else paid my rent? Did people really have jobs like this or was the idea simply too good to be true?

I spoke to a family friend who had worked at Club Med. His only question was whether leaving my profession now would make it harder for me to get a teaching job again later. I said, "No!" I could leave teaching to work with kids at Club Med and come right back, thinking I would be gone for three months or at the most, five or six.

I had a one-on-one interview at Club Med Sandpiper in Port St. Lucie, Florida, and the woman I met with asked me about Club Med Copper Mountain in Colorado.

"Wait. There's Club Med where it's cold?" I had thought Club Med was only on the beach. "I have scuba experience," I explained. "I want to go diving."

"I know, but I really need someone for the kid's program in Colorado," she told me. She was practically begging. "It says on your resume that you won a bronze NASTAR medal, so I know you can ski." I tried to wrap my head around the idea of freezing in the snow rather than swimming in the warm, Caribbean waters. She continued, "If you do me this favor, I promise that your next village will be sun, sand, and scuba." I was still not convinced, but she asked me to think about it over the weekend and call her on Monday.

I flew back to California. A few days later, I was scheduled to go on my very first overnight, liveaboard dive experience to Monterey Bay. I ended up completely, horribly seasick. When we motored back to land, the waves were even worse and I sat in the back of the boat in heavy seas throwing up over the side. I screamed as loudly as I could, "I am moving to the mountains! I am going to Club Med!" I sometimes wonder if that trip had been different, if we'd had calm seas and bright skies and I'd spent the day as planned swimming among the sea otters that floated on the surface and watching the sea lions, would I still have chosen to leave San Francisco and head east to Colorado?

I arrived at Copper Mountain with mixed emotions. Before I left, I kept busy and tried not to think too hard about what would happen next. While I wanted a new adventure, I felt sick to my stomach about all the questions I still had about my life and all of the What Ifs. But it was only for a few months. I was a great skier and maybe I could get back the feeling of living in Israel and in the dorms with people around who wanted to have adventures together.

Our job as a GO (Gentle Organizer) was to make sure that everyone who came to Club Med had a great vacation. The guests were called GMs, which stood for *Gentils Membres* (Gracious Members) and they were intended to be like family. Every GO had their own responsibilities in their own department. I worked in the Kids' Program and skied with the kids every day. And even though we all had different daytime responsibilities on the slopes or in the kitchen, everyone was in the show at night.

There were people who called Club Med "Club Bed" and for good reason—there was lots of sleeping around among the GOs and the GMs, and, in fact, it was encouraged. At the first weekly staff meeting I attended, our Chief of Village said at the outset, "Next week, there are going to be a lot of single women here and I want them to be happy." I thought to myself, *Dorothy, we are not in Kansas anymore.*

When I initially took the job, I'd had no idea there were performances every evening and that I would be required to be in them. My first show was a dance show, and I was in the back. The team tried to teach me the dance numbers to no avail, and even though I was not very good, I was thrilled to be in costume dancing on stage. I was however excellent in "The Dating Game" and my character, Marge, who was a very nerdy librarian was often chosen as the winning date.

At the end of the ski season, our village shut down and I transferred to Eleuthera in the Bahamas. Club Med had turned out to be the perfect place for me. When I was living in San Francisco, I missed having people around who wanted to do something active. Being at Club Med was like working at summer camp all year round—somehow, I had turned my favorite childhood memory into a job where they not only paid me, but also sent me to new, exotic places.

As at Copper Mountain, in Eleuthera there was a lot of foot traffic to the bedrooms. I still felt out of my element in this regard, but my college friend, Heather, who was feeding an infant every few hours, told me to think of it as a man scavenger hunt, a treasure quest for 31 Flavors of Men. "Sleep with someone with a beard. One with a hairy back. You can have sex with anyone you want," she told me via fax. I decided to test the waters.

One friendly GO named Tanner started sitting with me at dinner and for drinks and then one night we walked back to his room and he put a sock on the door, just like in *Dirty Dancing*. I finally had sex at Club Med just like everyone else.

If you completed two contracts at Club Med, you were allowed to ask to go to any village in the world for two weeks, as long as you paid your own airfare. I put in a request for two weeks at Sonora Bay on Mexico's Pacific Coast. When I arrived at the stunning village situated on the Sea of Cortez, I signed up for scuba diving all day, every day, and could not wait.

While I was there, I spoke with a few guests on vacation from working on cruise ships. The way they described it, it seemed like Club Med, except they moved from place to place all over the globe and the staff was forbidden to eat or drink at the bar with the guests. It sounded like heaven. I didn't want to have to answer the same five questions at every meal anymore. I was hooked on being paid to travel the world, see new places, and dive in far-off locales.

My parents had a travel agent friend who knew someone at Princess Cruises, and when I returned to Los Angeles, I called for an interview. It turned out that a Kids Club GO job on cruise ships—what they called Youth Staff—was double the pay I was making at Club Med.

Sailing the Seas

At Thanksgiving a few months later, I boarded my first Princess Cruise. I grew up watching *The Love Boat* television program on Saturday nights, and never imagined walking onto one of their ships just like Julie McCoy, but here I was on the giant white ship with my brand-new uniform. The ship was enormous, with more than a dozen decks and music and people everywhere. I wondered if I would ever find my way around.

Right away, it was very different from Club Med. The crew area of the ship was a maze and people seemed to give directions in code: Follow the M1 and go to safety training. Go to the Purser's office and sign onto the articles. I kept smiling and nodding. Everything seemed bright and shiny and perfect. I wore my uniform—a blue polo shirt and white shorts—and went to the opening night meeting at the Kids Club for introductions.

One father asked me, "Is this your first cruise?"

"Yes, how can you tell?"

"You're more excited than the kids."

Having come to ships from Club Med, I had a slightly different perspective on how things worked. At Club Med, you were never, ever off. You worked in your service during the day and in the shows at night, and at mealtimes you were still interacting with guests. To me, cruise ships felt like a vacation. You never ate with guests, there was a separate bar for crew, and if you weren't scheduled, you had free time. If the ship was in port, the kids' program had to be closed, so we were always off-duty in port, except when we had In Port Manning (IPM). The rules of the ship were that one-third of the crew must always be ready for any emergency, even when alongside, so we took turns being on IPM and the other days we could go exploring.

There were a number of moments where having worked at Club Med did prove to be an advantage. On my first cruise, I was told by one of the more senior crew members to meet near the bridge at 9:00 p.m. for Fog Watch. I had a feeling this was a snipe hunt. They gave us hard hats and whistles and told us it was important to sound the alarm so the whales wouldn't run into the ship in the fog. The other new crew members were very anxious to do a good job, but I looked up at the sky to watch the stars. It wasn't foggy. And whales don't run into ships or care about fog. When they sent the crew out to sound the whistles attached to their bright orange life jackets, I stayed behind, and when the officer of the watch confronted me, I told him, "I worked at Club Med. I've seen a snipe hunt joke like this before." They laughed and told me I could take off my hard hat.

Sometimes it was the passengers who were clueless, and we often joked about the questions we got asked: "Do these stairs go to the back of the ship?" No, they go up and down just like at home. "What time is the midnight buffet?" (This was actually a fair question since it started at 11:30 p.m.) And one of the most popular: "Do the crew live onboard?" Once, just for my own amusement, I answered, "Nope, we come back in the morning with the helicopter that brings the newspaper."

The craziest question I ever fielded was from a woman on a cruise in the Mediterranean who asked, "Is this the same moon I see at home?" I couldn't even answer.

Fortunately, the crew member standing beside me jumped in and said, "Yes, ma'am," with a straight face, and the woman thanked him and walked away. I had an answer that would have likely gotten me written up or fired about arriving by airplane versus spaceship. Good thing I kept my smart-ass mouth closed this time.

The best part of working on ships was the people onboard. I have often described living on cruise ships as being in a college dorm where no one has any homework. In fact, we had no chores at all. My food was prepared by the ship's kitchens. I had a cabin steward who cleaned my room and took my laundry back and forth to be cleaned. We occasionally went ashore to pick up snacks, but there was no grocery shopping or stopping at the dry cleaners, or getting gas for the car, or any of the other things on a regular adult's to-do list. There were no bills to pay and when we weren't working, we were playing. As a result, I made many close friends who stayed in my life for decades afterward.

My first roommate on Princess Cruises, Zoey Jensen, had worked in the kids' program at both Royal Caribbean and Princess so she knew her way around. She knew what all the acronyms like IPM meant, and she taught me how to navigate ship life.

I had been told that when I joined ships, there was no more hanky-panky with guests and no more eating with them either. It turned out we ate in the Officer's Mess where we ordered off the passenger restaurant menu and could eat in the passenger buffet. There were times when we could eat in the main and specialty restaurants as well. It was the best of both worlds. And since the crew on ship was far more people than any Club Med village and from many more nationalities, the "dessert" buffet of men continued.

Another one of my best friends on ships was Dev, he was a member of the production (or video) team who filmed every activity and event on the sea days and made a videotape that passengers purchased at the end of the cruise as a memory, and one of my favorite scuba dive buddies.

When I was working in the teen center one day, I was supposed to show a movie during the afternoon. For some reason, I couldn't get the video system to work. I called Dev for help. He tinkered around and finally a movie came onscreen—except that we had just gotten pay-per-view onboard and what came on was the flesh-pounding, screaming, money shot of a XXX movie. Dev and I both threw ourselves in front of the television and tried to press all the buttons to make it stop, but it felt like time had slowed and the movie went on for hours, although in reality it was only several seconds.

We looked at each other and Dev said, "We are so fired."

But I looked at him and said, "Maybe no one saw."

Then one of the girls in the room called out, "Can you put that back on? It's way more educational than what they show us in sex ed."

I wrote up a report to the captain, hotel director, chief purser, and the office describing how the Teen Manager and Director of Video Production had inadvertently, for several seconds, showed XXX porn to teenagers on board. I was sure there would be consequences, but in retrospect, they probably laughed at my carefully worded letter. Needless to say, we did not have pay-per-view onboard for very long.

As I sailed with Princess and other cruise lines from St. Maarten to Skagway, Alaska, and from San Francisco to Kyoto to the Panama Canal, I always found ways to make my dreams of seeing the world a reality. I always asked for things nicely. While I was on a contract, I would often write to the office back home and tell them that all was going well and talk about my ideas for the next contract. I might say, "The Caribbean has been great, and I was in Alaska last summer, do you think you have a spot for me in the Mediterranean?" Sometimes they wrote back "no," but with an alternative. "We cannot send you to Europe this summer, but would you consider Australia?" Often their next idea was better than my first. Over the years I was able to work my way across the globe and have many terrific adventures. I climbed Dunn's River Falls and explored caves in Jamaica, visited the Catherine Palace in St. Petersburg, and got permission to leave the ship for three days in Peru to make the incredible trek to Machu Picchu. I even went dry suit diving in the frigid waters of Juneau, Alaska, where the instructor, when I asked him about gear and protection for my cheeks, said, "Once your face goes numb, you won't notice."

Over time, I had many relationships, and sometimes while I moved between cruise lines in search of ever-better itinerar- ies, I would run into the same friends, less-than-friends, and friends-with-benefits. On every contract, there were various men I took home from the crew bar. Most of my romantic relationships felt like my library books—I picked them up for an evening or a port or two but didn't hold on to them for too long. As at Club Med, there was a crazy amount of sex happening on these ships among the crew. Relative to what was going on around me, I felt like a prude. But when I returned to land and saw my old friends, I felt like I was the wild one.

At one point, on a phone call with my sister, I told her, "I think I must be deaf."

"What are you talking about? Why do you think that?"

I said, "Because I'm thirty-two years old and my biological clock must be ticking, but I absolutely do not hear it."

Ultimately, I lasted seven years on the high seas, working my way up from Kids Club Manager to Cruise Staff, to Loyalty Ambassador, and even to Senior Assistant Cruise Director for Renaissance Cruises, until they went bankrupt eight days after September 11. I switched cruise lines to get better pay or more interesting itineraries and collected experiences across many continents. I loved that during the night my house moved, and I would wake up somewhere exotic. Plus, I was being paid to be there.

And yet, as amazing as all of the ports, men, and experiences were, one morning I woke up and opened my curtains and thought to myself, *Are we here again?* I knew then that this was my final contract. Anyone who can wake up and look at the gorgeous island of Grand Cayman and feel disappointment needs to go home. In many ways it was hard to leave the industry, but I believed in my heart that I could find other ways to travel.

It was a hard choice to leave ships, mostly because there was always a part of me that kept thinking, *just one more contract, one more continent.* But the writing was on the wall, and finally "one last contract" really was the last one. At age thirty-seven, I moved home with my parents and back into my childhood bedroom (little did I know I would be back there again in my forties).

Working on ships allowed me to travel to six continents and truly made me feel like a global citizen. I practiced languages, learned about cultures, built my scuba diving skills, and walked cities in far-off places from Muscat to Tallinn.

On the School Yard

WWhile I'd received a Master's in Education and had years of past experience, when I left the cruise ship behind, I didn't have all the requirements to teach in a public school. I thought earning new credentials might help. I began taking classes at National University in Sherman Oaks, where I was able to work on both a single subject credential—science—and a multiple subject elementary school credential, which would allow me to get a Studio Teacher's license.

I needed to student teach to validate my new credentials, and I wanted practice, so I agreed to an interview for a job teaching eighth grade science in the Culver City Unified School District. I met Patti, the principal, and a seventh-grade teacher. They seemed very interested in me.

"It's too bad you can't hire me," I said. "I would love to work with you."

Patti asked, "What do you mean I cannot hire you?"

"I still need to student teach."

Patti told me she could certainly offer me a job, and that I could student teach in my own classroom on a waiver, get paid, and have it count for all the hours needed.

I would be teaching four sections of eighth grade science which included chemistry, physics, and family life, or what we used to call "sex education." And I was rusty. When the head of my department asked me for a full inventory of the classroom, I stared at the equipment and couldn't remember the names of the beakers and Erlenmeyer flasks. I was certain this was a huge mistake, but school started within days, so I fought the urge to hyperventilate or throw up in the closet.

Earlier in the summer, I had interviewed to be a religious school teacher at my synagogue, Stephen Wise Temple. By the time I had the offer from CCUSD, it felt too late to quit the job at the temple, which meant I would be working six days a week: Monday to Friday at CCUSD and Tuesday afternoon and Sunday at the temple. I also had a volunteer job at the Long Beach Aquarium as a safety scuba diver on Saturdays. In a flash, I had gone from having nothing to do to working every single day. On ships, I had worked seven days a week, but my commute had been by elevator!

Teaching middle school in Culver City turned out to be a far cry from the cozy preschool world. I cared about my students and felt like I was making a difference in their lives, but I was exhausted. I had moved out of my parents' house and gotten an apartment that I liked, with an outdoor space for plants, and I could walk to some restaurants. But with teaching all day and my weekend job at the temple, sometimes I would sit down on the couch and fall asleep as soon as I got home from work.

I had a few dates and occasionally people set me up, but nothing in the romantic department was working either. It was different from being on cruise ships where I'd had breakfast, lunch, and dinner with the same people and we knew each other so well that we could order for each other from the menu, and there was a new supply of eager, available men with every contract. In comparison, the real world was lonely, and being an adult and paying bills, buying groceries, making lunch, and having chores paled in comparison.

As a treat to myself, I started to eat ice cream for breakfast on Saturdays. My favorite flavor was Häagen-Dazs's Chocolate Chocolate Chip, and I would eat it on my couch, straight out of the carton while watching reruns of shows from my youth on television. I felt proud of myself for eating only half the pint as if it was a sign of restraint and strength of character. I started slowly gaining weight. I didn't have a scale and was not focused on how I looked.

In the spring of my first year at CCUSD, Curtis School (my alma mater) contacted me about teaching the following year. Financially, there was no way not to accept the new job offer, but I still had misgivings about leaving my kids behind. Shortly before I had to decide, my incredible principal announced her promotion to superintendent, which made it clear that I was leaving CCUSD.

From the moment I set foot on campus, working at Curtis was a whole different experience. At CCUSD, it had been a challenge to get the parents to come to school for any reason, even for back-to-school night or conferences. At private schools, teachers usually complain that it is impossible to get the parents to leave. But I immediately loved the parents and the community. Since I would be the science teacher for grades DK through third, I now had three hundred kids' names to learn, which made the 150 at CCUSD seem like small potatoes.

Even though I was busy with school, I tried to date. I was on Jdate and sometimes would have a first date but never a second one. One time my friend Betty from high school and I went speed dating. There were ten men and the same number of women. You sat in a chair and when the bell rang a different man sat down across from you and you had three minutes to talk and make a connection. After four or five men, I was not even sure who I'd met. I tried to write some notes—red shirt, glasses, film editor—and for one, I wrote LIAR! Afterward, Betty and I talked about who we'd met.

She asked, "Did you like the guy who was in love with scuba diving?"

"You mean the LIAR?"

"What happened?" she asked.

I told her the "scuba diving guy" who was supposedly in love with diving had only done it once and he really knew very little about it. When he talked about diving, I'd been so excited, as meeting someone with the same passion as me would be fantastic. But when I asked him where his favorite place was to dive, he said he had done one try-out dive in Mexico but never finished the course because it was too much time away from drinking on the beach.

Eventually, I figured that I would spend the money for the matchmaking service, We Make Matches. It seemed perfect. They handpicked dates for you from an exclusive network, and you went to lunch—no pressure. Someone from the service was your helper and guide, and it was all going to work out perfectly.

I went for my initial interview and the woman said, "No problem, we can definitely get you a man in your age range who is a non-smoker, went to college, and lives nearby." Soon after, they called me to set up my first date. I went to the restaurant in Beverly Hills and waited. When my date was fifteen minutes late, I started to wonder if I had been stood up. After about twenty-five minutes, a man arrived. I had his name but no photo or contact information, and his first words were not, "I'm sorry I'm late," but, "Can we sit outside where I can smoke?" I should have simply left but it was lunchtime, and I was hungry, so I stayed. He was cute to look at but clearly crazy. He talked about being in France and shipping gun holders back to the USA to sell. I thought to myself, *He was late, he smokes, he runs guns. What kind of thoughtful process at We Make Matches made them think of him for me?* I looked directly into his eyes and asked, "Where did you go to college?"

"I didn't even finish high school," he scoffed. "I wouldn't waste my time on college."

I wish I could report that I said, "Check please," and walked away, but in fact, I sat with him and let him be charming, and even let him walk me to my car and kiss me because, let's face it, I was bored, and it had been a while since anyone kissed me.

I called We Make Matches to complain.

They said, "We are learning your preferences."

I responded, "What is complicated about the criteria 'went to college' and 'non-smoker'?" They claimed my date had lied to them. I was willing to give them another chance. They promised the next man would be much better.

A week later, they called me with another date. He was a music professor and did not smoke. I went out that night with my friend Naomi and she said, "Listen, when he arrives and he is an after-school guitar teacher in kids' homes, I want you to say, 'Excuse me,' and call me from the bathroom so you can hear me laughing from miles away."

I went to the restaurant at the appointed time and waited. After twenty minutes, my date showed up. He did apologize for being late. I said, "Were you teaching at the university today?" He looked at me quizzically and said, "I teach after-school guitar lessons to kids." When I excused myself to call Naomi from the bathroom, as predicted, she could not stop laughing.

"But how did you know?" I asked her. I did stay for the date, and he was fairly nice, but I was angry about being taken again by We Make Matches.

A few days later, I went to dinner with my friend Dafna who was an assistant district attorney. She said, "What you are going to do is send a letter demanding a full refund." I told her I'd already requested a refund, but they didn't offer them. She said, "This is the next step. Send the letter and wait for their reply. After that, I will help you file in small claims court."

As predicted, We Make Matches sent a letter back confirming they did not give refunds. I followed Dafna's next steps to file. Soon afterward, I received a FedEx package. I opened it, and inside was a letter which was highlighted, in bold and underlined in red. The letter was from a senior producer at *Judge Judy*. They wanted to try my case on television.

I called my sister who is a lawyer in New York. She said, "Absolutely not. Do not go on that show. They will make you look like you are crazy." But after working on ships for years, I wasn't afraid to look a bit crazy to get We Make Matches on the program. I wanted them to have to answer for their poor work practices no matter how I looked.

"As long as they look crazier!"

I called the producer whose name was on the letter. I offered her the direct line to the We Make Matches team in Los Angeles. I figured that would help them find the right person to go on television with me. She told me we'd talk again in a few days, and I was all set to tell her about the arms dealer and the guitar teacher, but very soon after that I received another FedEx. This time, it was from We Make Matches and it contained a check for my full refund. I was happy to have the money back, but a little disappointed about missing my fifteen minutes of fame with Judge Judy.

Around this time, I had a fight with my doctor. I was no longer having ice cream for breakfast on Saturdays, but I was so busy at

Curtis that I wasn't very active and when I felt lonely and dateless, dessert was my very best friend. I went in for a check-up and she commented, "Lisa, you have gained quite a bit of weight."

To which I promptly said, "No, I have not. All of my clothes still fit."

She countered with evidence and facts from my chart. "Look here," she said, "This was your weight a year ago, and six months ago and now." The numbers were right in front of me, but I was having none of it. I was angry. How dare she bring this up? I was upset, but also embarrassed. I left in a huff.

Over the next few days, I thought about the last time I'd gone shopping and how some of my older clothes seemed to have shrunk in the laundry. I realized I rarely looked at myself in the mirror. I thought about how lots of people wanted to go on a first date with me but not a second date after they saw me, and maybe I didn't look so much like my old photo that I was using. Maybe my doctor was right. My first plan of attack was to stop gaining weight. The scale should stop going up.

I began keeping a journal of my food and my daily weight. I thought more about what I ate and what I bought, and the fact that I taught three hundred kids and it was always someone's birthday at school. At first, I thought, *It's rude to not participate in the party!* But then I thought about my elastic pants. I had to make some changes. I focused on decreasing my calories and increasing my exercise. I stopped eating cake for everyone's birthday and started walking during recess with my students.

In December of my second year at Curtis, I went on a cruise for New Year's Eve with several friends. We had a lovely time together and we all shared our resolutions for the new year. I announced that I had two: Find and buy a condo, because I wanted my own home, and meet someone for a long-term relationship. It was not my goal to get married, but I did want to spend time with someone important. I wanted to find someone sensitive, sexy, smart, funny, and fantastic. I wanted to meet someone Jewish—a doer who liked to cook and didn't smoke, who had a quick wit, was in my age range, liked to celebrate the holidays, and had hobbies. I wanted someone who loved to travel!

CHAPTER 8

Prince Charming

It seemed like my resolutions were starting to come true in early January of 2007 when I found a condo and put in an offer. That same week I had a second email from a man on a dating website who had written to me before. I told a friend this and she immediately said, "Get off the phone with me and write him back right now."

This man had written me back in October, but at the time, I was busy with school and not feeling great about myself, so I never wrote back.

Sender: ManofMusic
To: LAteacher
Oct 8, 2006 8:04 p.m. PST

Hi,

Very cute photo! I too work in the classroom. I am also an avid traveler, especially to South America and South East Asia. Have your travels taken you to either of these parts of the world? What position did you have on the cruise ship? Singer?

I definitely do NOT live to work and have many interests that might be in common with yours. Check out my profile. Where will your travels take you next? I'm off to Bali & Lombok over the X-mas holidays. Being new in the area, where are you planning on practicing your faith? I was at the temple on Main Street in Santa Monica for Yom Kippur.

Take care, Fred

Now, several months later, he had written to me again.

Date: Jan 9, 2007 9:57 p.m. PST

Hi. I was wondering where in Belize you did your project. I just returned from Indonesia where the divers were involved with a program that placed metallic frameworks beneath the ocean. They attached coral to the framework and then ran an electric current from a generator to the structure. The end result should grow reef 10x as fast as coral would grow naturally. The most impressive one that I saw was a huge underwater dome that should be amazing once the coral fills in the framework. The efforts are due to improve upon what the bombing fisherman did to the stunning reefs, now illegal, thankfully. Did you see any of this in Belize as well? For which district do you work?

Now that I think about it, I think that I wrote you once but you never responded...maybe?

Anyway, hope to hear from you this time...that is, if this is a second time.

This time I did write back to Fred, the handsome Peace Corps worker and teacher. We started emailing back and forth and he was engaging and entertaining. He seemed to check a lot of boxes on my list. We made plans to meet. As he said, "There are not many travelers like us out there, no? At least very few that I know of."

When Fred and I met at the bar, it was the first time I'd heard his voice. We had never spoken by phone, but his voice, when I heard it, was comforting. He was a bit shorter than his profile said but cuter than his photo. He was dressed smart in chinos and a shirt with a collar, which put him heads above most guys I had met up with. He gave me a quick hug and suggested I take the view of the water and sunset. But I was so enamored of our conversation, I never even noticed the picturesque view shining behind him through the nearly floor-to-ceiling windows. We had tea, and then neither of us wanted to leave so we decided to share a burger.

When he took out photos of children he had met while traveling in Indonesia, I was in shock. A man had brought photos of his trips to show me! He took pictures, he shared, he talked about travel. He seemed like he really wanted to connect. In Los Angeles, no one seemed very interested in my past adventures beyond the most basic level, or my desire for more exploration. He felt like a kindred spirit.

When he showed me his photos scuba diving at Biorock in Indonesia, I learned more about the underwater structure designed for coral growth and protection that he had described in his emails. I'd never been to Indonesia but wanted to go. He liked scuba diving and traveling. I felt like I was dreaming. Had I created this magical man who liked the same things I did?

At one point, he asked me, "What is your favorite place?"

I immediately responded, "The Shwedagon Pagoda" with no other explanation. The Shwedagon Pagoda is an ornate temple complex in Myanmar that is one of the most visited sights in the country, but few people have heard of it. The square is the size of a New York City block, full of carved stone structures with marble snakes curling up the staircases. It is the most sacred Buddhist pagoda in the country.

Fred responded eagerly with, "What about Bagan? Did you not like that more?"

Bagan is another ancient city and temple complex in Myanmar that was the capital of the kingdom from the ninth through the thirteenth centuries. He was astonished that I could have been to Myanmar and not seen Bagan. When I explained I had traveled by ship and had only gone where the ship stopped, Fred was adamant that I needed to go back. He made it seem like heading back around the world to see Bagan was as easy and natural as popping down to Ojai for the weekend. I said I wanted to go. And I secretly started imagining that maybe someday we might go there together. Even if it didn't work out, I thought, Bagan was added to my list of places I wanted to see. Since he worked with kids, Fred knew the dramas and challenges of being an adult in a school setting. We didn't talk much about work, but I implicitly felt very understood. He was animated and impressive. His intelligence was apparent. He was Jewish. The conversation just flowed, and without discussion, we both canceled our plans for the rest of the night. He called his brother to cancel their plans to watch the game together, and I was supposed to meet friends to go dancing, but I called from the bathroom to say, "Go without me. I am staying here!"

Eventually, he walked me to my car. Not only did he kiss me, but he also asked me out for a second date! I wasn't left wondering if he liked me or not; he wanted to go out again. The curse of First Dates Only was broken.

For our second date, I met Fred at his house near Venice Beach before we went out to dinner. The online dating rules say you're not supposed to go someone's house too early, but I felt like I already knew him. His Bohemian home fit with my idea of the poor teacher-slash-former-Peace Corps worker who didn't care about material things. I met his cat, Bob Dylan. Fred told me he'd named the cat after his favorite musician and joked, "I wanted to get a voicemail someday that said, 'Bob Dylan is waiting to be picked up.'"

Fred made me feel welcome with many kisses and said he wanted to kiss me all night. I asked about his guitars, which were all around the apartment. He had studied at "Guitar College" after high school at the Musician's Institute. I told him I had two guitars at my house and wanted to play better. He offered to give me a few lessons—more things in common, more ways to connect. After an hour of making out, we walked to a nearby sushi place where we ordered sake, chicken teriyaki, and tempura and spent the next two hours talking about his time in the Peace Corps—travel misadventures as well as some of our next travel dreams.

As we talked, I was happy to note that Fred didn't seem threatened by the fact that I was smart. Fred had been to university several times for multiple degrees, which I took to mean he was smart and curious about many topics. And although we had met online, it turned out we had many connections. Fred, my mother and I had all worked for the same woman doing educational therapy. One of Fred's best friend's cousins was my classmate from high school. The house he'd grown up in was very close to where I had grown up in Los Angeles, and if I'd gone to public school, we would have both been at University High School. We joked that we would never have liked each other in high school. I was way too nerdy, and he was far too "band cool." As our conversation continued, we found even more connections, and things seemed rosy.

We returned to his place after dinner for more making out. As we snuggled on his couch, I felt something on his arm like a Band-Aid. When I asked him about it, he ripped it off his arm and threw it behind the couch. It was a smoking cessation patch, and it seemed like he felt embarrassed, or maybe he was concerned I wouldn't date him if he was a smoker. Fred had tried many types of substances over the years but claimed not to use them currently and I believed him. I was giddy that a hot man was interested in me, one who showed me photos of his trips to Indonesia, and worked with kids and played guitar. When he kissed me, I felt like I was finally the star in a romantic comedy. Someone wanted to kiss me more than leave to go out to dinner. He wanted to be with me. I'd had so many bad dates and waited so long for someone who was looking for the perfect travel match. Even if it was only these two dates, I felt happy and crossed my fingers there would be many more.

On our third date, I was nearly late, and I am never late for anything. I'd had to sign papers for the offer for my condo. I loved the condo in Brentwood, and if I wanted it, I had to act quickly. It was my first time buying a property and I had no clue about all the paperwork, inspections, and other matters to handle. I was excited and overwhelmed and returned to my apartment with only moments to get prepared for our evening out. I was getting dressed in a brand-new dress I bought for this (a third) date at the Grove, and I rushed to the door when Fred arrived. I felt almost dizzy with anticipation for the night ahead, as well as the possibility that I might own my own place.

As I closed the door behind me while we walked out, I stopped in my tracks and realized I had left my keys in the apartment. I told him I had never done this before. Whenever I am going out, I often double- and triple-check that I have everything with me.

I turned to him, took a deep breath, and said, "New plan. Instead of going to dinner in Westwood, let's drive to my parents' house. I can get my spare keys and we can eat at Paulo's restaurant."

I was worried, but Fred was relaxed and said, "No problem." He seemed flexible. I liked that.

We drove twenty minutes to my parents' house and they weren't home. I found the spare keys and we drove across the street to Paulo's, which happened to be one of my favorite restaurants. The owner is a family friend and he treated us as VIP guests. Fred was very impressed.

We started to see each other twice a week, on the exact same two days a week, Tuesday and Sunday. I was not sure why only these two days, but before we would leave, we always made plans for the next time. I went to temple on Fridays and made plans with friends or worked on lesson plans the other days. I didn't want to rock the boat and did not bring it up, but I thought it odd that it was only ever those days. During the week, the rest of the days, we barely spoke by phone or email, but we were both busy with work and I always knew when I would see him next. At one point, I joked with Fred about how he had a different girl on the other days of the week. He didn't see any humor in this. It was still early, so we hadn't talked about or defined our relationship, whether we were exclusive. We hadn't slept together yet. I wanted to, but I wanted the time to be right and I was careful not to put pressure on anything when everything seemed to be going well.

One weekend, my young adult group from Stephen Wise Temple had arranged a local hike. I invited Fred because I wanted him to meet my friends, and I wanted to see what other people thought of him. The terrain felt steep to me and I found the hike challenging. I was still working on walking more but had clearly not graduated to hills. Yet Fred was encouraging. At one point, I said, "I think I'll just stop and stay here. You can visit me on the weekends. I can't go up anymore." Fred laughed and said I could rest and then we would keep going. He spoke with the young rabbi and my friend Naomi, who had counseled me through many bad internet dates. Everyone wanted this to work out; they wanted me to be happy.

I wanted to lose weight and be in better shape, and Fred loved to hike and knew all the trails around Los Angeles. One weekend, he drove me to Malibu, and as we were walking, we saw a wolf on the trail. It felt magical. He regaled me with stories of trekking in Nepal with one of his friends. I wondered if I could ever do that. Could I walk for days with a pack on my back? Would I want to? Would I get to have sex along the way? I was very interested in having sex again. I was very interested in Fred. His interest in me as a travel partner was intense. He seemed to be looking for someone to go exploring with him, and he was amazed that I liked to do what he liked to do. I had never considered trekking in Nepal. It was so far out of my comfort zone that I would have sooner thought to travel in space. Now it seemed like a possibility.

Early on in our dating, my parents invited me to an event at our temple where Elie Wiesel would be speaking. I asked if they could also get Fred a ticket. It was too soon to introduce my parents to my new sort-of-boyfriend, but Fred's dad had survived the Holocaust and although Fred was somewhat disconnected from Judaism, I thought hearing Wiesel might be something that would interest him. Fred was indeed interested, but nervous to meet my parents so soon. My dad said, "Listen, tell him we won't look at him or speak to him. He can just sit next to us. If he wants to go, we'll get him a ticket."

Unfortunately, on the day of the event, Los Angeles traffic was unsurprisingly heavy and Fred got extraordinarily frustrated on his way to meet me at the synagogue. He stopped at a café and had a bite to eat and called me to say he probably wasn't coming. I was disappointed, but he did rally and show up for the event. The microphone at the podium wasn't working properly, and while it was hard to understand every word, it was amazing to be in Wiesel's presence. Fred did speak to my parents, which I considered a win, and they were thrilled to meet a Jewish man who was interested in me.

After the event, I drove Fred to his car, as he had parked up the hill and we wanted to spend some time together without my parents. We made out in my car until all the windows fogged up. Our relationship was getting hot and heavy. My co-teachers at school told me to stop counting dates and start counting the months. I loved being able to share my temple and my family with him. It seemed like we were on a good track with our relationship.

We kept hiking and I was making progress each time. I no longer felt like I would die at every step and actually began to notice the beauty at the top. After one particularly hot and sweaty weekend hike, as we finally finished the long loop back to the car, Fred looked at me and said, "I think you earned a Slurpee."

"That sounds great. What's a Slurpee?"

In complete astonishment, Fred exclaimed, "You have traveled all over the world and you have no idea what a Slurpee is?" He was nearly ecstatic at the thought of introducing me to 7-Eleven's best creation. I wasn't sure how many times I had even been in a convenience store. I cooked and I shopped, but I had never eaten fast food growing up, and I still didn't. However, I fell absolutely in love with my Coca Cola-flavored 7-Eleven Slurpee. He also couldn't believe the trails and areas of our city that I had never explored, and the restaurants I didn't know. While it was true I had grown up in Los Angeles, I left when I was seventeen for Penn and had only recently started living there as an adult. He was happy to be my tour guide.

Fred's love of music was deep, and he was always asking me if I knew this band or that, and which concerts I had been to. My first concert as a teenager was Rick Springfield's, and I loved it when he sang "Jesse's Girl." But, as much as I liked it, I had never been to another concert. Once, when Fred and I were driving, his friend called and asked about the concert tickets he had recently gotten. She didn't know I was in the car and argued that he should bring her to the concert and not his new girlfriend who knew nothing about music. They'd met in school and often spoke in Spanish. I didn't speak as well as them, but I understood most of their conversation. I knew they were both into music in a way I would never be, but he did pick me for the concert! It was Sting and The Police, and I realized I knew many more of their songs than I thought; I just didn't always know that the songs I loved were theirs.

My parents traveled frequently when I was growing up, and so had Fred's when they were both alive. He told me about how, after his father died, he had taken care of his mom during her cancer treatments. He seemed a bit lost and lonely without either parent. He felt orphaned. Both sets of our parents had played bridge, we decided to take bridge lessons together at the same place his parents had played. He loved to go to the restaurants near his parents' former condo because it reminded him of when they all went together. He was also very focused on his friends from high school who remembered his family.

While Fred was generally kind and supportive, especially about healthy food and exercising, he was not willing to use condoms, so I was not willing to have sex with him. As the weeks went by and our relationship progressed, this became a problem. I was on the pill and told him to get tested for STDs and then we wouldn't have to use condoms. I had already been tested.

"I don't want to get tested," he said.

"Okay, don't get tested," I responded.

He was frustrated about not going all the way, but I felt good about setting a boundary, especially about sexual health, and that he had listened to me. I figured that eventually he would get tested. When he finally did, I chose to believe him, although in retrospect I wonder if he ever really did, because I never saw a printed report or screenshot of the test results. I wanted to have sex with him. I was completely in love with the idea of him and falling in love with him. Our physical connection was intense. We could not keep our hands off each other.

Fred was constantly planning travel and had a three-week spring break from school coming up at the same time that I would be taking possession of my new condo. He would be traveling to the Perhentian Islands in Malaysia and he made it sound incredible. I was jealous about his trip and nervous about him going away without me.

While he was away, I packed a box or two at my apartment every night and hired movers and taught school and tried not to worry. I loved my new condo and did my best not to imagine him sleeping with every bikini-clad girl who passed by. We emailed a few times, and I offered again to pick him up at the airport when he returned, but he said no. I was terrified that this meant he was done with me, but my friends all counseled me to let it go. When we were reunited, we discussed his trip and he said he missed me the entire time. I felt reassured that even though I didn't hear from him much, he was thinking about me while he was away. I didn't like how it felt for him to be away and for me to be left behind.

After Fred returned, he started talking about travel plans for the upcoming summer. He wanted me to join him in Fiji and Vanuatu for six weeks. It sounded exotic, erotic, and like the perfect place to do plenty of scuba diving, which we both loved. I was ecstatic—I had a hot man who loved to have sex with me and wanted to spend the summer in the Pacific Islands with me.

My friend Isabella expressed some concerns. "Do you think the two of you could go away for a weekend before you travel for multiple weeks in foreign countries?" I had to admit that this did seem to be how most people did it. I talked to Fred, and we planned a weekend in San Luis Obispo, which is a three-hour drive from LA and has wine tasting, hot springs, hiking, tide pools, and beaches. Unfortunately, nearly everything that could go wrong did.

We took my car because it was a convertible, and Fred offered to drive. On the freeway, he suddenly, and without warning, pulled into the emergency center lane. I asked, "What is going on?" He seemed like he was hyperventilating or having a panic attack, or both. He then told me that he did not like to drive on the freeway. This information seemed late at this point. I was perplexed because he had asked to drive, which I was happy to agree to, but now it made no sense at all.

We changed places and I started driving, but it took quite a while for him to regain his color and demeanor. When we arrived at our hotel, our room smelled and there was a dog barking loudly next door. Back at the front desk, we requested another room. The second room was an improvement in the smell department, but there appeared to be dogs everywhere.

I figured we needed to reset our day and we went for a walk on the beach. I spoke to Fred about my weight loss. I had lost twelve pounds since we'd started dating. I was proud of myself.

With a smile, I told him, "Now, I am skinny."

He said, "No, you are not skinny."

He was right. I was not skinny. I had more weight to lose, but he was unkind. A better boyfriend would have said, "You look perfect to me," or, "I don't care, I can't wait to get you into bed," or even, "Twelve pounds is great, good job." I cried myself to sleep that night because my feelings and pride were stung. I was not putting on sexy lingerie.

The next morning, I was quiet and concerned. This trip was not going how I planned. We went to a wine tasting, but I was focused on the calories and not on the flavors. Our next stop was to a hot spring, where we were supposed to soak and relax. But after his comments, I felt uncomfortable in my bathing suit and around him in general. He seemed oblivious to why I was in a foul mood.

Fred kept saying, "This is why I want to go to Asia. The people are more interesting. No one here is even talking to us because we're just another boring American couple. It will be so different. The hotels are cheaper and the sights are more interesting. And we'll do really cool, adventurous things like meet an orangutan in Borneo."

But we never talked about how it would still be the two of us. No matter where you go, you bring yourself and your problems with you. It did seem like a different kind of trip might be better for us, and everything he said convinced me that this destination was the problem. I began to overlook what was actually happening in hopes of things being better somewhere else. I knew everything might not always be perfect, but I wanted the relationship to work. And I really, really wanted to go to Fiji and Vanuatu with Fred.

When we returned to Los Angeles, Fred was on good behavior. He went to dinner with my friends and their children, and he even went with me to services on Shabbat. He seemed to want to participate in Jewish activities. For Tu Bishvat (New Year of the Trees) services, we were each given a tree seedling. We talked about growing the trees together and how it was a symbol of our relationship. It needed care and shelter continuously; you could not forget to water it and think it would grow and survive.

I'd been looking into dance classes for a while, and when Fred agreed to participate in a beginner's salsa class with me, I was thrilled. I had taken many types of dance lessons over the years and always danced swing with my dad at any event. We had a great time at the first class; we smiled and laughed. Fred even agreed to go again. This time I invited my friend Isabella to join us. When we arrived for the second class, Fred told me he wanted to go in the intermediate group this time. I asked him if he was certain, and he emphatically said, "Yes!"

During class, Fred left the circle of dancing couples and went to sit down. We'd rotated partners, so I was dancing with someone else when I saw him sitting on the bench by the door. I was unsure why he'd left. The intermediate class was more challenging than the beginner's but I was keeping up. He didn't look hurt or upset, and it was only a forty-five-minute class. I wanted to soak up every second possible. I kept dancing.

When class ended, Fred stormed over to Isabella and yelled at her, "You need to take Lisa home."

She looked at him and said, "You need to discuss this with Lisa."

Fred turned to me. "Go home with Isabella!"

I was still out of breath from class and completely bewildered by his behavior. I asked, "What's wrong? What is going on? You're leaving?"

"Why didn't you check on me?" he yelled. "I could have been hurt or sick, and you never even checked on me. You just kept dancing and smiling at the other men."

"Fred," I said, trying to remain calm, "I am not going home with Isabella. My car and my keys are at your house."

"Fine," he stammered. "Let's go."

When we got to his house after a very quiet ride, he told me to get my things and go. I went inside and gathered up my belongings, but I refused to leave. "We need to discuss this."

"If you won't leave, I am leaving," he said, and slammed the door to his house, got into his car, and drove off.

I managed to get into my car and drive a block down the road before I burst into tears. I pulled to the side of the road and called Isabella. She said, "I am not sure what happened at class tonight, but I am also not sure if you want to be part of all this drama."

I didn't want to be part of drama. I did not. But I really wanted to go to Asia and to Borobudur Temple in Indonesia which had been on my bucket list for years and years since my early cruise ship days when a friend spoke about it in glowing terms. I was falling in love with him, or the idea of him, or of what we might be together. When Fred wanted to be charming, he really, really was.

I spoke with him about my concerns from the dance class and he listened to me. He did not apologize for his behavior or promise to change but I felt better for saying my part. I focused on our upcoming trip and spending the summer with Fred in Fiji and Vanuatu. I was swept up in the excitement. For so long after I left ships, I had worried I'd never travel again. Fred was the map to the next way. I had a new condo and a teaching job I loved, and Fred was convinced we could travel wherever we wanted.

For the rest of the school year, I walked more and more each day and lost weight slowly and sensibly. Fred was available more and more. I saw less of my friends but told myself that it made sense. I felt like my New Year's resolutions and my life goals were coming together. I was about to turn thirty-nine and thought, *I am happy, this is what I wanted.*

I did keep my little tree that I received at Tu Bishvat services alive. Fred's tree died, but my tree lived and then we called it our tree. Looking back, there was a message here about all the work I was putting into our relationship versus how much he was putting in, but I wasn't paying attention. For the moment, I wanted to hold onto him as tightly as possible and not let go.

CHAPTER 9

A New Vision

When I first returned to Los Angeles after I left Fred, a friend advised me it was impossible to do new things in old ways. I wanted to move forward in my life, and I seized upon any new experience that anyone recommended: salsa dance team, hula hoop lessons, kickboxing classes, and every kind of therapy imaginable. I tried medical hypnosis and Core Energetics and went to Radical Aliveness weekend retreats where I pounded on blocks with tennis racquets and ran around the room screaming. I drew my feelings in bed while watching movies and then ate my feelings in chocolate and ice cream. I also tried working with a couple of traditional therapists, but the sessions were always over phone calls or Skype, and I finally decided that I needed to see someone in person. Eventually, after many referrals and attempts, I met Connie Kaplan.

When I was thirteen years old, at a regular appointment with the optometrist for my glasses, the doctor recommended that I see an ophthalmologist. He couldn't correct my vision to 20/20 and was concerned there might be an underlying issue.

We went to the specialist who told my mother, "I also can't get her to see 20/20, but there doesn't seem to be a medical issue." It was clear that I didn't have a tumor or a malformation, but no one thought to question how this problem with my vision might be impacting my daily life. No one asked me about sports or our family history, which included my dad's strabismus, a condition in which the eyes do not properly align with each other when looking at an object. I believed what I was told: that I was clumsy and unathletic.

Connie was a therapist who was also a teacher of Eye Movement Desensitization and Reprocessing, EMDR, which is related to rapid-eye movement therapy. EMDR uses bilateral taping as one part of a phased-focused treatment to unlock negative memories and traumas and then detangle them as part of the therapeutic process. I had been referred to her by the medical hypnosis person as a way to rapidly move trauma out of my body. During our intake session, I mentioned the eye issues I had experienced throughout my life. In my early forties, around the time I was first dating Fred and working at Curtis, I had finally been diagnosed properly with esotropia, commonly called a "lazy eye." Connie gave me a referral and I went to see Dr. Alan Brodney.

From the first tests he ran, Dr. Brodney could tell I had trouble with the vision in my left eye and agreed I had left intermittent esotropia. While I couldn't see very much in 3D, I could still see a bit, which meant my brain had not entirely turned off the feed from my left eye. I told him I was terrible at catching a ball and parallel parking and had trouble with right and left—especially in dance class—got lost a lot and could not understand the instructions for two hands centering in art class. I also mentioned my family summer camp experience in Santa Barbara when I was eleven. My age group's designated activity one day was a bike ride from the University area into town. I was in the middle of the group of bikes, and people kept passing by me and going faster. I was busy focusing on the riders near me and the front wheel of my bicycle accidentally locked onto the back wheel of the bike in front of me. That's the last thing I remember. I was later told that the boy in front of me had jumped off his bike, and my bike and I hit the curb together and did a backflip. I landed on my head. Back then, no one wore helmets. When I came to, I looked up and saw all the kids standing around me in a circle.

"Get back on your bike," the counselor said. "We're going back to camp." So, I got on the bike and rode back to camp. My parents took me to the emergency room where I had X-rays. Two hours later, I was released from the hospital. Fortunately, I was deemed physically okay but I was afraid of bike riding after that.

Dr. Brodney said, "That makes sense. Of course, those things would be challenging for you." Then he said he thought he could help me.

This was the first time anyone had ever connected the issues with my eyes to the everyday things that were hard or frustrating for me. If he was right, it meant I was *not* clumsy or unathletic. I had an eye problem. I thought about how students felt when they learned they were dyslexic and not stupid. It was exactly how I felt. The world was different. Maybe there was a reason I preferred to travel in certain ways and could not play tetherball at all.

I was intrigued.

I agreed to more testing. For my vision assessment, some of my scores were 1 percent, 2 percent, 9 percent, and 37 percent. I was confused. I figured it was out of 100 percent, but it just did not make sense to me—1 percent? I called Dr. Brodney to ask about my results.

"Is one percent a good score? Are you trying to have zero?"

He answered me kindly, "Lisa, just like on every other test you have taken in your life, one hundred is a good score."

"But how can this be true? I have a Master's degree in Education."

I was taken aback when he responded, "Lisa, when I see scores like yours, I am just happy that you can read."

I thought to myself, *Houston, we have a problem.* I read more of the report. It said that I had "difficulty" with my "ability to assemble parts together to form a complete picture" and that it was a challenge for me to "attend to an image (accomplishment) while ignoring the background." It also said I struggled with the "ability to understand that objects of varying sizes have the same meaning" and noted that "poor visual closure" might cause me to perceive an object "as many small pictures rather than as a single picture."

"I cannot believe my scores are so low," I said to Dr. Brodney.

He responded, "This is an opportunity for you to figure out more about yourself. You have intermittent left esotropia, which means your left eye turns inward. Some people call this lazy eye, and it means there is a problem with how your eyes align and team to work together. This is a functional vision issue involving your eyes and your brain and how they work together for you to interact with the world. When your eyes do not team properly, the brain is challenged to combine images from both eyes in a 3D image. Intermittent issues can cause more symptoms, including poor depth perception, eye pain or strain, blurry or double vision, headaches, difficulty catching and throwing objects, clumsiness, and squinting. It causes a reduced ability to perceive, and certain types of skills are missing in your toolbox. Scores like these would qualify someone for a learning disability. But you've adapted. In fact, you've adapted remarkably well. However, if you have the desire to try to improve and are motivated to improve, it is likely that I can help you. If you attempt this, you'll be able to notice things you never noticed before. It will be easier for you. Things have been hard." Then he smiled and said, "I can promise you that you will be better at sports." Dr. Brodney explained that sometimes the brain turns off the feed from one eye. If that was the case, if I saw no 3D at all, vision therapy could not solve that. However, since I did see limited 3D, vision therapy could help. My brain still received the feed, but I would have to retrain both my eye and my brain.

I started to think about how many times I just could not do things right. In art class, I was looking but I wasn't seeing. I couldn't understand the perspective the instructor was asking me to take. I wanted to follow her instructions, but I simply could not do it. I remembered being in a dance class, and when the teacher was near me or directly in front of me, I did great. But when the teacher moved to another part of the room, I had to translate right and left in the mirror and I couldn't figure it out. I had always been challenged by right and left. I always felt so dumb. How could someone who could blow the curve at an Ivy League institution not know right from left? Now, I knew why. Parallel parking, my bike accident, my near drowning at camp, my terror on the ski slopes when the light changed. All of these things made sense to Dr. Brodney.

"It's been hard for your eyes to work together," he told me. "It's been hard to see in depth, and harder to discriminate. You have challenges in making judgments and finding things. You've had to compensate."

I realized that I hadn't even considered how my vision issues impacted other areas of my life. It was true I had trouble finding things. I remembered at the end of freshman year when Teresa asked me to leave my own room. I asked, "Why am I leaving my room?" and she said, "You asked for my help to pack this suitcase. The only way to help you is to start over and take everything out. I think it will upset you. It might be better if you just leave." It was true that I always had trouble packing. I was concerned I would take the wrong things, that I wouldn't have what I needed when I arrived, and I could never figure out how to get everything inside the case.

After the visit with Dr. Brodney, I made charts in my room and gave myself a sticker for every time I went to vision therapy. I also got stickers for doing my vision homework every day. I tried to think about it like brushing my teeth—it didn't take very long, and it didn't seem to be doing that much, but it was necessary to do every single day. And it was deceptively simple. But it was hard for my eyes and brain to understand what it was that I wanted them to do. Read with this prism or say these letters out loud. On the computer, I had to click on certain things depending on the exercise we were working on. Sometimes I had to stand on a mat and follow the directions to move in certain ways. Quite a few times I left the session and burst into tears. I couldn't do what they wanted me to do. Well, I could do it, but I had to put in extraordinary effort and afterward I often needed a nap. My brain was so tired I couldn't even read or watch TV. It felt like after years of guessing how to make the edges of things come together, we were ripping it all apart and beginning again from scratch.

I started to get more work opportunities to travel, but I committed to being in Los Angeles three of every four weeks in order not to miss too much vision therapy. I took notes at all my sessions because what I had to do with all the different charts and tools was confusing. But I never gave up. The plan was to do three sets of ten sessions. After my first ten, I was re-tested and Dr. Brodney said, "I can tell that you've been working hard and I'm impressed with your improvement. I didn't expect to see this much change already." He suggested I think about taking tennis lessons. I was incredulous.

"Like that won't be frustrating," I muttered.

"You need to put your new skills into action. You need to challenge yourself to do things that you couldn't do in the past. You have to decide to apply yourself."

I picked my tennis teacher, Perry, because he was recommended by my neighbor, an elite tennis player, and also because he mainly worked with children. I figured my skills were at or below a seven-year-old's. I explained to him in depth about my eye issues and that I wasn't sure I could play.

At one of our first lessons, Perry said to me, "Lisa, what is it that you're watching? Because it's not the ball." We discovered I could find the ball much better to my right than to my left, which made sense, but never imagined that my serve would be fairly good. I took lessons once or twice a week for several months and my ability improved greatly.

After many sessions, Dr. Brodney told me, "For the first time since I've seen you, your depth perception is at a normal level. It's easier for you to achieve it." This was a giant goal and huge progress. He continued, "Now we just have to keep it stable and get you quicker at using these perceptual skills, at making them automatic." He was glad I was taking tennis lessons, but he wanted me to do more. What did that mean? He suggested challenging myself. I wasn't sure what that meant. I thought about a drawing class or more dance. I realized why I had always sat in front of the classroom growing up. It was easier for me there, with less distractions, and I always sat to the right of the room. He also wanted me to work on my memory. I was supposed to work on being able to draw my route from home to someplace I often went, from memory. With directions I often felt lost, and even though I rarely *was* lost, that feeling was enough to make me turn around and go home.

At every session, Dr. Brodney reiterated that my goals were to try not to shut down, but to try new things, challenge myself, and build up my confidence. I realized why my therapist had thought this was such a good plan. Not only was I getting therapy for my eyes, but actually for my whole life as well.

After a year of vision therapy and thirty sessions, I was invited to come in once a month and do my exercises on my own every day. I went once a month for another year and then went down to once a quarter.

The physical act of seeing had always been a challenge, but through my sessions with Dr. Brodney, I came to understand that "seeing" is also about recognizing or understanding. My eye issues had made me miss things that were happening around me, like when a ball hit me in the face as a child. But I began to wonder if they had also made me overlook or fail to process signs that were clear to others but not to me. Or made me unable to put all the pieces together—including the warning signs in the early days of my very flawed relationship with Fred.

Perhaps also because of my eye issues, I believed in working hard, in the value of overcoming no matter what. I persevered at school despite my obstacles, and I succeeded. I fought through my terror on the ski slopes as a child and was rewarded with a medal, and later a job. The one lesson I didn't learn until much later was that sometimes struggle means something fundamentally isn't right, and that fighting for it or working around it is not the answer.

Worth More Than Two Pigs

For our first international trip—which was really our first trip anywhere for more than two nights after our terrible weekend in San Luis Obispo—Fred and I flew to Fiji and Vanuatu for the summer. There were some amazing highlights in those three weeks. I went diving on the SS President Coolidge, the world's largest easily accessible wreck, to 140 feet, which I was trained and qualified for and had done once previously on an instructor dive off the cruise ship. I had my first "bucket bath" in a tiny village with no running water, limited electricity, and a Peace Corps worker. And over kava one night, Fred and a local man decided that I was worth more than two pigs.

The flipside—the one I tried to pretend wasn't there, the one I didn't share with anyone, not even my family and friends—was that from the moment we landed together in Nadi Airport, we were fighting. I was in tears at the baggage claim. During the flight, I hadn't liked the meal, so I ate the bread and butter. But Fred shamed me about eating butter because he was worried that I was going to gain weight. After his comment on the beach in San Luis Obispo, I had continued on my slow path of weight loss and didn't discuss it with him again. I was walking more and hiking with him. I was less lonely and not making poor food choices. On the plane, it was simply that I was hungry and didn't like the food. Was he really just a jerk? I thought maybe this trip was a mistake. Maybe my friends who were concerned were right.

I took myself to the bathroom and thought about getting on a plane right back to Los Angeles, but it was my summer vacation too. I didn't want to fly home and have no summer vacation. I was in Fiji for goodness' sake. Was I really never going to touch Fijian sand? Should I give up now? Every couple has fights, right? I wanted to scuba dive and relax and enjoy myself. I washed my face and returned to the baggage claim, determined to discuss this with him. I explained my feelings and he apologized. I wanted this trip to work out so badly. He did seem sorry.

We left the airport and went to Port Denarau to get a ferry to the Yasawa Islands, but it turned out you couldn't board the boat without a confirmed stay at one of the islands. It was very early in the morning, but the staff quickly helped us confirm some of the places we were considering. Fred liked to show up and figure it out, including how many nights, but that was simply not how it worked. He was aggravated about not being able to just get on the boat. I was impressed with how helpful the team was since clearly this was not how it was done, and they really wanted to assist us to get on the next ferry. Finally, we got on the big yellow ferry, which looked like a school bus, and went from island to island. Canoes or small boats from the individual islands would come out to meet the ferry and bring you to their resort.

We stayed at very low-budget locations with food not really to my liking, as Fred believed in staying local and cheap. He craved the hostel life where people interacted more and shared tales from the road. It was the pure *Lonely Planet* philosophy. He thought overpaying for a luxury property where no one wanted to chat was doubly bad. I understood that if you paid less for accommodation, you could certainly travel longer on the same budget. It was true people talked more in hostels, especially when strangers were all sharing one room!

At one of our stays in the Yasawa Islands, I went scuba diving. Fred was in a bad mood when I went diving. He was a diver, but he thought it was far too expensive. I was paying my own way, so I couldn't see why he had an opinion about how I spent my money. I loved scuba diving, which he knew when he met me, and I found his reaction confusing. Each time I set out for a dive excursion, he made it very clear he did not want to go, he did not want to spend the money, and he did not want *me* to go. He made this clear again when I came back. As the days went by, I tried not to let his gloom overtake my excitement about diving in the clear Fijian waters. Sometimes Fred would snorkel while I was out but, mainly, he would pout.

Vanuatu was even further off the typical tourist trail, and it was a wild experience for me. We didn't stay in a hotel but in a local village where people mainly spoke French. Fred didn't understand how I'd never had a bucket bath and I couldn't really understand why we were staying in a place that had nearly no electricity and no running water. But he was excited for me to experience village life. He had a long talk with the Peace Corps volunteer and felt in his element. Fred didn't feel like my time on ships was "real" traveling and I could see his perspective better being in these circumstances. I still maintained that I had traveled for years, but simply in a very different style.

In Vanuatu, we chose to go to two islands. Fred really wanted to go to Tanna, a third island, to see the active volcano, but the inter-island flights were pricey and we decided that would be for another time. On the island of Santo, not far from our French village, was one of the most famous deep dives in the South Pacific.

We dove for two days with the shop started by dive pioneer Allan Power.

The instructors and dive masters said I could go not only deep alongside the SS President Coolidge, an American troop ship which had sunk during World War II after sailing into two mines, but also swim inside to see "The Lady." Fred was fairly good-natured about doing the shallower dive and he had zero interest in going to the very deep depths or penetrating a wreck. It was within the scope of my training and past dives yet still a tinge scary. My two dive buddies took great care of me and it was a day of diving I will never forget.

When we returned to Fiji, Fred's friend Gregory from Los Angeles was also in the islands at a wedding, and Fred had arranged to meet up with him. But I was never told before we left that he would be spending my final week with us. I was on a three-week trip and Fred was staying several additional weeks. I had met Gregory a few times. He and Fred both loved music and Fred had sold Gregory one of his keyboards or a guitar amp, which was how they first met. The first night we were together, Gregory was distressed at dinner and told the story of why he was upset. Sitting next to me and across from Fred, I patted his arm like I would to soothe a preschooler in my charge and said something like, "That sounds upsetting." He was one of Fred's best friends and I wanted to be supportive.

Later that night, under the moonlight in a hammock, Fred started yelling at me because he believed I'd been hitting on his friend. I was in complete shock.

"You invited him on our romantic Fijian getaway. You did not tell me we would be spending a week with him! I cannot believe you are mad at *me!*"

I was in tears and again devastated and confused and wondering if I had made all the wrong choices. Later that night, Fred told me, "You are perfect. I didn't even know I was looking for you. Will you travel with me for a year in Southeast Asia?" Everything was so muddled. He was angry at me. He wanted to be with me. He was screaming at me. He was inviting me on an adventure where I could see my dream destination of Borobudur in Indonesia that I first heard about when I worked on cruise ships.

Back in Los Angeles, I sought the advice of friends and talked through my concerns about this travel proposition. Betty said, "You have an American passport and a platinum credit card. Let's say you go and it doesn't work out. You can come back. What if he goes without you, will you wish you went?" That was fairly compelling. I could always leave and come back.

Friends from my cruise ship days were wary. Julie asked me, "Can't you just go away for three months each summer? Why does it have to be a year? You love your new condo. What are you going to do with it?"

Fred had answers for every concern. For my condo: "Wouldn't it be great, if we were in Asia and someone else was paying the mortgage? You'd have the equity and the photos of our trip! Seems like a win-win." He even offered to help me find a tenant. When he left every summer, and even for three-week holidays, he sublet his apartment. We started to talk about him moving in with me. I still had concerns about his behavior, but I was excited at the thought of being away again. *Maybe*, I thought, *this could be perfect.* Fred loved to hike and adventure, and we could work on our relationship. He was going to take me places that I knew I could never travel to alone. Hopefully, we'd fall more deeply in love.

Fred was able to get a one-year leave from his job, but when I asked Curtis about this option, they said that if I left and they hired someone else they would not wait for me to return. Fred was convinced this wasn't a problem. His friend worked at another school and he thought they might be interested to hire me in a year. I met with them and they said to keep in touch.

We started to look for tenants, I thought about my work options, and then we went backpack shopping. I had a total and complete meltdown in the backpack section at REI. I could not pick one. I couldn't fathom holding all of my things for a year in a backpack that I couldn't lift. I was overwhelmed and nearly hysterical. Fred looked at me calmly and said, "Just take the bags you brought on our trip to Fiji and Vanuatu." I probably should have paused to rethink why I was upset, but I kept rolling with the plan. I was going traveling with a man I loved, who said he loved me too.

I had never really been interested in getting married, but once I fell for Fred, I wanted to be married to him. We were giving up our jobs and our apartments and running away together. One day, when we were walking along the canals in Venice Beach, I asked him about getting engaged.

He said emphatically, "No. I am not getting engaged so you will go with me on this trip. If you want to go, I want you to, and that is all."

"Our culture has no other way to have a formal public commitment. I want you to declare that you love me in front of our family and friends."

"I love you."

"I know," I said. "But I want you to say it in front of other people and formally."

He took a bow as people walked by and said in a formal voice, "I want you to come with me to Asia."

I wanted to go with him to Asia, but I also wanted to feel committed as a couple. He said he loved me, but wasn't interested in getting married. I was enjoying our time together. I wanted to travel full-time again. Who knew if he would change his mind? Maybe I would change my mind about him.

I took Fred as a work in progress. I knew he wasn't perfect. I knew *I* wasn't perfect. He had started dating me at my absolute heaviest. We were always at each other's places now and seemed to be building a life together. He made going to Asia for a year seem easy. I wanted in on his adventure.

In order to go on the trip, I needed money. Fred had the savings for a year-long adventure. One night at dinner in Fiji, somewhat randomly, he asked me about signing a prenuptial agreement, which was a shock because he had been adamant that he did not want to get married. When I asked, he said he didn't want me to take his family money if things didn't work out.

"I would be happy to sign a prenuptial agreement," I said. "Please get it from your lawyer and I will have mine look at it." He never brought it up again. To pay for the long trip, I decided to generate some extra cash by running a summer camp at school. Simply Science Camp was a huge success. The kids and parents loved it and I made enough money to fund my trip.

Fred asked me if I wanted to write a book about our year away together. I was all in with the idea, but I wasn't sure if we were good writers, or if our trip would be interesting to anyone else. In the back of my mind, I was also worried—what if we didn't get along? Would that be in the book too? I agreed to keep a journal, even though I already kept one, and Fred agreed he would keep one too.

Before we left for Asia, it made sense for Fred to give up his apartment and move in with me. He was giving his car to a friend and my parents would keep my car at their house. Our plans were coming together. It was really happening. We had booked tickets to Papeete, Tahiti, French Polynesia, to depart on July 31, 2008. Immediately after he moved in, we started to look for tenants and make the condo ready for a renter.

Right after we listed the condo, I got a call from a woman who wanted to come over as soon as possible. They'd been searching in the area and had seen many dirty, sub-par, small apartments. She needed a one-year sublet for her daughter and wanted a one-bedroom. She would be teaching at Archer School, literally a block from my condo. Her mom loved that I was a teacher and Fred was a teacher and that my parents weren't too far away either. They were willing to take it at the rent we had listed, and the dates were just about perfect as she was coming for the school year. They were ready to sign a lease that day.

We put our things in storage, moved our cars, had the carpets cleaned, and got our bags ready. My parents drove us to the airport and hugged us goodbye. I promised to send emails when we landed so they would know we were safe.

We were flying from Los Angeles to Papeete to start our adventure. I had been to Papeete, but Fred had not. As our flight descended, Fred turned to me.

"Do you want to get married on this trip?"

I was astonished, but I said, "I love you," and he said, "I love you too."

CHAPTER 11

Paradise Adjacent

Fred and I did end up writing a book about our year in Southeast Asia. Written after our return, it tells a story very different from what actually transpired during our eleven months together. It's filled with picture-perfect descriptions of all the incredible things we did, like biking in Bagan, going on a van tour of the Gobi Desert, and scuba diving in Thailand—all interspersed with fervent, near-constant pronouncements of our love and respect for each other, and in particular, of my gratitude for Fred and all his amazing qualities. It does not describe the trip as it was, but as how we wished it to be. For a long time, that was how I chose to see it.

We did have some wonderful times. I remember going to Saba and Sarawak in Malaysian Borneo and seeing orangutans with their babies in the Sepilok orangutan sanctuary in the rainforest. Off the coast of Borneo, Fred and I went diving at Barracuda Point on the island of Sipadan with hundreds of barracudas swimming in a column that looked like a tornado.

In Nepal, we were in Tansen, in the middle of the Himalayas, where there were very few Westerners and fewer restaurants. The first night we bought *momo*, the national dish, around the corner from our guest house, with the man who functioned as tourist greeter, hostel owner, and honorary mayor. It was more someone's home than an actual restaurant, and they were teaching us Nepalese. On our second night, I thought I asked in Nepalese for chicken momo, but the family looked at me askance. I asked again. It turned out I had asked for dog momo, not chicken. *Kukur* is "chicken" and *kukura* is "dog."

In China, I was finally able to use my wordless book that I had carried for months in case we couldn't communicate. I figured if I pointed at the different pictures, we would be "talking." In Kunming, which is in China's southern Yunnan Province, we saw three men grilling meat in front of a shop. We approached them and I pointed to "cow," "pig," and "sheep." One of the men pointed to the cow and said *"Chigha."* I told Fred, "This isn't so hard. Now we know cow." We went into the shop to buy ice, and I pointed to "ice." The shopkeeper also said *"Chigha."* I said to Fred, "The same word cannot be both cow and ice." Then a very helpful man behind us in line said that *chigha* does not mean cow *or* ice, it means, "This one!"

There were many language mix-ups, although I did my best to learn as many words and phrases as I could and to communicate to some degree everywhere we went.

I did better with Indonesian, Bahasa Indonesia, because it required no tones and had been mostly invented in the modern era as a unification device. There were so many islands, tribes, and languages in the world's largest archipelago that Bahasa Indonesia was created to "give" to the country to simplify things. I loved that *jalan* meant "street" but *jalan jalan* meant "walking." *Timor* means East, which means that when people say East Timor, it actually means East East!

Thailand was our favorite place, and as the year went on, we moved in and out of Thailand all the time. I loved the people, the food, and the smiles, and on Bangkok's backpacker areas of Khao San Road, we could apply for visas, have our teeth cleaned, and get local knowledge from other travelers.

I always told Fred I was his sidekick, but after we'd been traveling for a while, he said no, I was also a superhero. When he was positive, he lauded me for my superpowers: (1) I was psychic: I knew when people were trying to scam us; (2) I had Sticky Fingers: I found things and picked up useful pamphlets, maps, information, and flyers; and (3) I was great at networking. I would chat up the man at the travel desk in the tourist office and get a great deal on whatever boat or bus or attraction we wanted to do next.

Fred was adamant we only stay in very inexpensive accommodations, for budgetary reasons as well as philosophical ones. He said it was a better way to travel. The people were friendlier and you got great local tips, which saved us several times when a traveler coming from the opposite direction knew solutions to make the next part of a trip work. Sometimes we would meet up with these people on purpose or sometimes accidentally on the backpacker trail, and it was like a family reunion. While I couldn't argue with the fact that we had more friends and better advice, I was often less than thrilled with our quarters. The rooms we stayed in tended to have lumpy mattresses, thin walls, limited lighting, and nearly no curtains.

Sometimes the travel itself was arduous. After we left Sipadan, we went to Derawan in Indonesia, a remote chain of thirty-one islands. Getting there required many forms of transportation and us carrying all the cash we thought we might need. There were no banks or ATMs on the islands and they didn't accept anything but cash. At our hotel, the owner would show us the fresh catch and we could walk on the main street into a "restaurant," always part of someone's house, and they would cook it for us. One day, he took us to the nearby island Kakavan, which was over an hour's boat ride away. Along the way, he stopped and told me to put on my snorkel and mask and hold the rope. It was a new sport to me; it felt a bit like water skiing because I was holding the rope, but I was underwater watching the fish go by. He was a crazy skipper, so I mainly hoped I would live. On our next stop, we walked along wooden planks on the island to an interior lake where there were supposedly stingless jellyfish. I wasn't sure I believed it. There were more jellyfish in the lake than flowers in a summer field. Either I was going to die immediately, or it would be awesome. We were the only people there, and once I realized I would live, I enjoyed it immensely. I was proud of myself. I did it. I did not let the fear win.

My biggest fear before we'd left to travel for a year was that without any planning ahead, we would have nowhere to stay and be homeless. As we moved around, we paid attention to when there were festivals or holidays so we wouldn't be trying to find accommodation somewhere at a time when it was crowded and impossible. One time in Bangkok, while waiting for a visa, we decided to go to Koh Samet, a popular island. On a Sunday night, we thought all the visitors would have left since they would need to work on Monday. It turned out that it was a three-day weekend, and when we arrived, people on the beach told us to get back on the small boats because there was nowhere to stay. Fred said this likely wasn't true, that we'd already paid for the boat to get here and we should stay. We walked around, meeting many backpackers sleeping on the sand with sleeping bags, which we didn't carry. There were tents everywhere and every place we stopped at had signs that said FULL.

We went back to a bar near the docks where we'd arrived, and the group from our boat was at a picnic table drinking. They said, "Don't worry! This bar said we can sleep on their tables after they close up and they'll lock our bags in their office." I was not excited about this idea and thought we should get back on the boat and go somewhere else. But Fred felt that all the islands would be crowded. He reasoned that after one night under the stars, there would be plenty of accommodation as everyone would leave to go back to work. I had many worries, but I didn't get eaten alive by mosquitoes, the bar lent us many pillows to make the benches more comfortable, and we used our sarongs as blankets.

I kept in touch with our family and friends as we went, and each month, I spent time in internet cafés in the cities we visited, uploading photos and sending news of our adventures back to my former students. Their parents sent emails back sharing how much the children appreciated being remembered and learning from my enthusiastic newsletters. Fred felt I was wasting time and money, but it was an important promise for me to keep.

There were times when we did not get along, times when I wondered what I was doing in the middle of Asia, far away from literally everyone else I loved—and who loved me. I remember Fred yelling at me in the middle of a crowd, "You are no fun! What is wrong with you? Everyone is having fun but you." We were in Chiang Mai for Songkran, the traditional Thai New Year's celebration, and it did seem that everyone was enjoying the party but me. It was like a city-wide fraternity party from Animal House with water guns, barrels of ice-cold river water, and days of water fighting. It went on day and night on every street. At one point, I grabbed hold of a woman who had poured dirty, ice-cold water on my face and screamed at her. I wasn't sure I could take any more of the water wasting or the "fun." Fred had turned into Rambo and was loving it, however, and he made it clear that my bad attitude was ruining it for him. For my part, I couldn't wait for the "fun" to be over.

As the trip went on, it became clear that Fred's drinking was getting worse. There were lots of opportunities for drinking since he was always in vacation mode and focused on playing ukulele, the games on his phone, and reading the map to figure out where to go next. I only drank on Saturday nights. I couldn't drink daily and feel well. Fred would drink at night in our room, and no matter how much he drank, he was never hungover. He bought bottles of cheap Thai alcohol called SangSom that is 40 percent proof.

One night in Thailand on the island of Koh Lipe, we had many drinks with a couple we'd met. Fred was so drunk he nearly started a fight on the beach and could barely walk home...again. It was not the first time for any of these things, and generally he wouldn't remember much about the things he said or did.

We celebrated the second anniversary of our first date (January 18, 2007) at Casa Del Mar on that island of Koh Lipe. By this time, we'd been away for six months. Fred said he wanted to go scuba diving with me, which he almost never did. I thought it was impressive he was willing to make the effort to make me happy. Due to the strong current that day, there was no diving, but you could snorkel on the less windy side of the island.

Fred never wanted to pay more to rent fins and, at first, I wasn't going to as well, but I decided it wasn't smart that day and went back to pay for the fins. He didn't make his normal fuss about paying for extra things, like my fins, and we set out. After seeing the colorful coral heads and fighting the current for nearly an hour, I started to swim in. As much as I usually loved being in the water, I was ready to go back. Fred was behind me and began gesturing wildly for me to come over to him. I figured he had seen an octopus or a squid, or something fairly exciting, but I didn't turn back because it was choppy and I was cold. But he kept calling to me, so eventually I swam back to where he was.

When I got near him, I looked around and said, "What's up? I don't see any fish."

He said, "Keep looking."

I still didn't see anything. He motioned me closer and then pointed with his finger. I kept looking under the water for some amazing creature. Now I was very close to him and said, "I don't see any fish anywhere. What do you see?"

He kept pointing and soon I saw a ring.

"You found a ring?" We were snorkeling over coral heads and my first thought was someone had lost their ring.

Fred reached down into the water and picked up the ring.

"Lisa, these two years have been amazing. I never want to be without you. Will you spend the rest of your life with me?"

I kissed him. "Yes!" I put on the ring. It had a large pink stone and a silver band. It didn't exactly fit on my finger, but I didn't care about that at all at the moment.

We got out of the water and went to a spot on the sand where Fred set up a photo shoot for us. He used the remote setting on the camera to take a picture of him kneeling in the sand on one knee, asking me to be his wife.

"I never expected you to ask me to marry you," I said. "I want to be married to you, but you hate weddings."

"That's true," he responded, "but I know it's important to you and I want to make a formal commitment to you. I love you and I want to be with you forever." I hoped he meant every word.

As the evening went on, Fred kept drinking until he passed out. I woke up the next morning very disappointed. I told him I was upset that on the day he asked me to marry him, he picked alcohol over having sex with me. He apologized and promised to do better. As an excuse, he explained that the night before he asked me, he'd been anxious that I might not say yes and that he got drunk with worry. And then last night when I'd said yes, he felt overwhelmed by excitement and drank too much again. That drinking was his solution to any uncomfortable emotion concerned me, and perhaps should have concerned me more, but we were away. We were in paradise in Thailand, and deep in my heart, I did really long to be married to him. I was getting what I wanted so I figured I was happy.

I wanted to call my family right away to tell them we were engaged, but Fred was exasperated. Why did we have to call? Why did we need to tell them now? He had many reasons why we shouldn't. My parents were planning to meet us in Asia in just a few weeks to travel with us to Cambodia and Vietnam for two weeks. They loved to travel and they missed us so they were joining us on our year away to catch up. Fred thought we should tell them in person. While I liked the idea of telling them in person, I also knew they would want to know right away. He also thought we didn't need to tell *anyone* yet. He wanted it just between us, and while I could see that for the weekend, forty-eight hours was about all the respite I could imagine. Then, he begged me to just email and not call.

"Listen," I said, "if you're in the hospital or you're engaged, you have to call." I finally reached my mom and she said we would celebrate soon when we were all together. I also spoke with my sister and some friends. Everyone was excited for me, and I realized I hadn't spoken to any of them for so long. Fred didn't call anyone to share the news, but he said he emailed his brother earlier about his proposal plans.

We spent much of the next day working on a way to get my ring to fit my finger. It was too small, but I was certain a jeweler could resize it. At the first store, the owner asked, "Want to see a real diamond?"

At the second store, a helpful man informed us, "That ring cannot be sized since it is not silver. Would you like to see a ring in real silver?" Then he suggested we go to the silversmith at the craft bar on the other side of the island.

The silversmith asked me, "Why didn't you buy a ring that fits?"

"Can you size the ring or not?" I replied. He started to work, offering to make a new ring entirely and hammering the ring repeatedly, but it was still too small. As he continued to work, the stone fell out.

"Don't worry," he said, "I can glue that back in." *Great, glue away*, I thought to myself. No matter what he did, it was still too small.

Finally, I suggested he cut the back of the ring so I could wear it. After cutting the band and regluing the stone, my engagement ring fit. However, the edges dug into my finger, and the next day, my finger turned green. Fred suggested we have a new ring made in the same style. I tried hard to reassure myself that this was a reflection of the ring and not our relationship. But I really, really wanted the ring to work, just like I did everything else.

When my parents came to visit us, I expected it to be relaxing and fantastic. My parents had arranged for everything, and we would be staying in real hotels with air conditioning and fancy linens, doing our sightseeing excursions with a private guide. But Fred fought with me about everything. Our guide, Song, was supposed to meet us at the airport in Hanoi, Vietnam, when we arrived, and Fred was excited to have a sign with his name on it. But the guide forgot to come get us, and we ended up having to take a taxi to our hotel. Along the way, the driver pulled over to the side of the road and tried to change the price, but we were having none of that nonsense. We started to get out of the taxi on the side of the road and told the driver he would get nothing. The driver finally agreed to take us for the original price. When we arrived at last, we were both tired and irritated. After months of staying in places with barely hot water and sometimes no towels, I was thrilled with our luxury accommodations, but Fred continued to find fault with everything. He groused that the food we ate in the hotel while we were waiting for my parents was not that tasty and too pricey.

My parents arrived with the guide, who was embarrassed that he had not picked us up. It wasn't a good start for Fred and this guide. When the guide told us the plan for the next day, Fred said simply, "Impossible." He was used to making all the decisions and didn't want to get up early. My parents never had any jet lag, and on every trip we'd taken, they were up in the morning for the breakfast buffet. Fred and I normally stayed for at least three nights in any given destination, but that was not the plan while we were with my parents. They had limited time and wanted to see as much as they could. The guide tried to lighten the mood for everyone by jokingly calling Fred "Mister Impossible," and left us with assurances that we were going to love his itinerary and a reminder not to be late tomorrow.

Every day my parents were with us, we woke up early for a sumptuous hotel breakfast to start our day of touring. We had a large, air-conditioned vehicle and a driver as well as our guide, Song. On our own, the two of us would sleep until we woke up and go wandering, but my parents were ready to see as much as possible every day and fill every moment with knowledge and memories. One day, we departed the five-star Metropole Hotel in Hanoi at 8:00 a.m., and Fred was so unhappy and vocal about it. We toured the Hanoi Hilton where John McCain was a political prisoner during the Vietnam War, went to an ethnicity museum, and at night, to a water puppet show after a large dinner. I was thrilled for my parents' company and learning so much from the guide. I loved to go to museums and shows. Fred complained about everything: "Why do we have to get up before the sun? Why do we have to do so much in a single day? Why do we have to eat all these fancy, expensive meals? You're going to get fat again. Why are you having dessert again?" I reminded myself that being with someone twenty-four hours a day, seven days a week, was challenging. Of course, we would squabble. Traveling with someone else's parents is hard. Fred was having to adjust to my family and our ways, so I needed to give him more slack.

The trip did have its lighter moments. Fred and my mom had always gotten along well and he frequently asked her for ideas about his clients. But even now when they weren't working, they still found things to talk about. My dad, Fred, and I took a Tai Chi class at one of the hotels, and even though my dad protested, "I'm too old to learn this new stuff," we didn't give up, and by the end of our one-hour lesson, we were able to go through a series of ten movements with minimal assistance from our teacher. At a market in Cambodia, we shopped together for a pink stone to make me a new engagement ring. As the trip went on, Fred and my dad became Team Vodka due to their fondness for searching for Happy Hour drinks at the end of the day when our sightseeing excursions wrapped. When the two of them saw the broken clock in the train station in Dalat, they declared they could drink any time they wanted because it was always Happy Hour in Dalat.

Fred did freak out in front of my parents one day when we were talking about our future wedding plans. We were watching an online video of a wedding at Casa Del Mar, which was where we'd had our first date. He'd been the one to ask if we could get married there, so I couldn't see why he was so upset. It turned out he was upset because in the video, the groom's parents walked him down the aisle, and Fred's parents were both deceased. I felt awful. Here we were watching the video with both my living parents. We talked at length about ideas and options and Fred ultimately decided he would ask his aunt and uncle to walk him. He also wanted to play a song on his guitar while the cantor sang. He had many ideas. From our travels, we were able to pick out a color and flowers, and even learned to fold napkins in the shape of a lotus like those we saw at one of the fanciest Vietnamese restaurants. By the time my parents left, we had a date, a location, the clergy, and more ideas.

One night, my mom talked about having Sunday brunch after the wedding. Again, Fred flipped out.

"I'm allergic to mornings. I'm not getting up the morning after our wedding and seeing those people again."

I tried to be sensitive. We were traveling with my family. We were talking about our wedding. It was a lot. I cared more about being married than the one day, I kept telling him. But the brunch was very important to my mom. People have a brunch the day after a wedding, that's just part of the wedding weekend. Rehearsal dinner. Wedding. Brunch. There would be many out-of-town guests. They would need food. But he was getting more and more agitated, and then he screamed at me, "Your mom is insane! You are ruining the wedding. You are ruining our wedding night. I think we shouldn't even get married."

"We are not canceling our wedding because of a brunch," I told him.

On our last night in Vietnam, we were with my parents at the rooftop bar at the Rex Hotel in Saigon (Ho Chi Minh City). My mom was talking about making a guest list, and Fred was still going on adamantly about how he wanted the Five Fs: Fun, Formal, Fantastic, filled with Family, and no Friggin' early luncheons.

If my parents were concerned about Fred's hysterics, they discussed it among themselves. I kept chalking up any drama to the challenges of traveling 24/7 with others. We had taken a night train to the hill country in Vietnam and Fred skipped the most amazing tour walking through the local villages to sleep on the couch in the lobby of our hotel since our rooms weren't ready. They did mention that he seemed to need a lot of sleep. We had an early flight one day and I wondered if we would even make it. I was tired of his outbursts and glad when he chose not to go on every tour. I just hoped it was more about the stress of being with family and his inner turmoil of, as he called it, being "orphaned." I kept telling myself no one was perfect. Traveling together was challenging. He needed his space. My parents were happy that I was happy. I thought I was happy.

After my parents left, it was a challenge to return to our previous level of accommodations and travel style. Although we'd been in Cambodia for a week, I felt like we had just arrived. I had to get reacclimated to no air conditioning, no guide to whisk us to the front of lines, and no nice things like fluffy towels. I also missed my mom and dad. They were great to travel with, although being with them had highlighted how difficult Fred could be at times.

One night in Laos, I slipped in a bathroom at the restaurant where we were having dinner and hurt my back. The floor was wet and I'd slipped on some steps. While I wasn't seriously injured, I was in pain. Fred had been worried when I didn't return, but the next day we had an argument in the street because he was angry that my back hurt, that I was hot and tired, and that I wanted to get a tuk-tuk instead of walking three miles.

I said, "My back hurts, it is one million degrees here at high noon. Why can't we take a taxi?"

Fred shouted back, "You are gross! You are stupid!" His words felt like swords going through my body. He turned, and it looked like he was ready to walk away from me.

"Please don't leave me here," I begged him. I wasn't even sure where we were exactly or that I could find my way back to our hotel alone. Also, I never carried any money. Fred always had the money. Normally I paid more attention to where we were and how we'd gotten there, but today I just hurt.

He stayed, but he ignored me, and we stood around waiting for fifteen minutes, upset and angry. Eventually he kind of acknowledged me, and begrudgingly I gave in and we kept walking. Why couldn't we have taken a tuk-tuk? It wasn't about money. He wanted to win. I remember his anger; I could feel it like the steam that fogs your glasses after the hottest shower in a small bathroom. I couldn't see it happening, but I knew it was escalating.

I was also frustrated with myself for being in that situation. I knew I should pay more attention to where we stayed. It was one of the factors while we were traveling that made me feel more dependent on him. When I first had my eye issue diagnosed, Fred thought it was no big deal. He said, "I'm color blind and it never impacted me." But my eye issues affected everything. It prevented me from seeing his bad patterns. It was why I couldn't build the vision of the towns, and why that day in my distress I was completely unable to figure out where we were and felt even more dependent on him.

Earlier on in this terrible, horrible day in Laos, we had taken the pink stone we bought in the market in Cambodia to a local jeweler, who promised to remake my proposal ring from Indonesia in pure silver for twenty-five dollars. We left it there, and when we picked up the new ring a few days later, I thought it would be perfect. It was not. By the end of the week, the new "pure silver" ring had turned completely black. Did I start to think it was a sign? Nope. I thought I was allergic to my ring or it needed to be cleaned.

When we arrived in Luang Prabang, the ancient royal capital of Luang Prabang Province in northern Laos, I asked a jeweler to clean my ring and he said, "This isn't silver. This ring is made out of nickel." Then he added, "I am the son of the jeweler who made the crown for the King. I will make you a new ring in one hundred percent silver." We left him the ring and crossed our fingers. Fortunately, this third ring worked like a charm. It fit, it did not turn black, it did not turn my finger green, and the stone did not fall out. At last, I was feeling good.

When we were next in Thailand, Fred and I went to several fancy jewelry stores looking for a proper engagement ring I could wear in America. I loved the idea of wearing a pink stone, and since receiving my first proposal ring, I had read that pink was the color of unconditional love from the heart. Finally, I found a ring in yellow gold with a 3.98 carat pink sapphire nestled next to two 0.24-carat diamonds. Instantly I knew it was my ring. Fred said, "Let's look at some other ones just to be sure."

"I don't need to. This is the ring for me, just as you are the man for me," I said. I had fallen for him, and I was certain. I thought about the quote from Abraham Lincoln, "We can complain because rose bushes have thorns, or rejoice because thorn bushes have roses." I was determined to focus on the roses.

I rarely spoke to any of my friends on Skype, although I missed them very much. I tried to email, but Fred hated when I spent time or money on emails or creating the newsletter. If I had, perhaps one of them might have suggested that maybe this relationship wasn't so perfect, or that maybe Fred was not the person I wanted him to be.

Toward the end of our eleven-month adventure, I began to get tired of moving about. In a thunderstorm in Laos, I had an interview on Skype and received an offer for a teaching job back in LA. Fred had been on leave, and would be returning to the same sites. Our tenant was getting ready to leave, we had our cars waiting for us, we had a wedding to plan. But Fred wasn't tired, he was still searching for more. He discovered that it was cheaper to fly home from Mongolia than from Beijing. He wanted to go to Mongolia. I did not. We didn't know what language they spoke or if we needed visas. But once Fred had an idea, it usually happened.

We made it to Ulaanbaatar by train. As usual, we didn't take the expensive train, we traveled, as Fred liked to say, like normal people. This meant starting with a twelve-hour overnight bus ride from Beijing to Erlian. We left at 4:30 p.m. and were able to lie flat, but the bus was full of smelly feet and at the one or two stops, the only thing to look at was all the men peeing against the wall. But we made it. Next, we had a few hours' sleep in a very cheap hotel in Erlian after our 4:30 a.m. arrival. Then we took a short taxi ride to catch a bus (10:30 a.m. to 1:30 p.m.) to the Mongolian border town of Zamyn-Üüd. We had several hours to explore before our 5:00 p.m. overnight train. We bought tickets, paid to store our bags for the afternoon wait, and while it was considerably cheaper than the sold-out fast train, it took two nights. It costs $330 per person on the expensive tourist train, and we spent $110 for both of us.

We saw a breathtaking sunset over the Great Wall as part of our journey and the locals in our train compartment helped us get a taxi into Ulaanbaatar on arrival. After meeting with several tour operators, we chose a ten-day trek into the Gobi desert in a van. We knew there was another couple going. We hoped we would like them. We rented sleeping bags and gathered our warmest clothing, bought food that wouldn't perish, and set off.

Very soon, we were beyond the power lines and paved roads. Mostly, the trip was incredible. I saw my first moonrise. The landscapes were brightly colored and remarkable. Every night we stayed in a different ger, the traditional Mongolian tent-like dwelling, and one morning watched camels being sheared. We helped herd goats with one family. We learned a few basic words in Mongolian, such as *sain benou* ("hello"/"how are you") and *mush sangh* ("very pretty").

Fred picked a fight with me for sharing food with the other couple. I actually just gave them some of our raisins and ate two of their cookies. He took me around to the back of the van and said, "If you don't watch what you're eating, you'll get fat again." This was not only unjustified, it was absurd. We were living on oatmeal for breakfast and ramen for lunch. We ate dinner at the ger, but there was often not much to eat. I didn't know it then, but the next month when we returned home, I would discover that I weighed just 110 pounds. I had lost so much weight that none of my clothes fit. We were literally in the middle of nowhere and he was upset I had eaten two cookies from my new friends? I felt defeated. Did he only care about my weight? We hadn't showered in days, there was no running water, we were in the Gobi Desert with dunes to walk on, where only a few resilient flowers somehow grew, and he wanted to fight about a cookie.

One night we stayed at the Ger Hotel in Dalanzadgad, where we had electricity but still a pit toilet. Our first stop was at the public shower house where Fred and I had a room together to shower. Instead of enjoying the clean water, we had a fight. Fred decided to stay in that night but I went out. Oggi and Bulga, our translator and guide, checked four bars before deciding on the Sand Bar, where I danced and tried to focus on all the good things, on all the amazing places we had been and the things we had seen.

After our adventures with the van, we went for three days to stay in a lodge in Gorkhi-Terelj National Park. The first night, the power was out and we ate in the restaurant by candlelight. It wasn't great, and for the rest of our stay, Fred made our meals in a hot pot. He made Cup O'Noodles soup, macaroni and cheese, oatmeal with raisins, and pasta with tomato sauce. We also snacked on cheese and dried fruit.

One afternoon, we went on a hike. Somehow, we got separated and I just stopped where I was. I remembered in high school we went on a trip to Yosemite and they said that if you get lost, stay put. But he never came back for me. Finally, fighting an urge to panic, I made my way back to our lodging, where the staff let me into our room. I could tell Fred had been there because he'd changed his shoes. I decided to sit outside on the porch and wait. When he finally returned, he was breathless, upset, and carrying wildflowers he had picked for me. He said he'd searched for me for hours.

"I was going to cancel my flight and search for you all summer. If I didn't find you after summer, I was going to move to Thailand. I cannot go back to Los Angeles; I cannot go home without you." He seemed earnestly upset. I knew we'd been separated on our hike, but I also knew how to get back to our lodging. I was never in danger or really lost in the wild. It felt a bit like a performance, but I was glad he searched for me and felt it was more about our trip ending and how lost he felt about our impending return.

I was excited to be heading back to the United States. Yet even on the plane to Los Angeles, we couldn't stop talking about other trips we could take. There were many places to go, and I felt like with Fred, I would see them all. For now, we were going home to work and save money, get married, and see what would happen next.

Down the Aisle

When Fred and I returned to Los Angeles, I was looking forward to starting a new job teaching K–6 science at Brawerman, a private Jewish elementary school, and planning our wedding for December with my mom. We moved back into my condo, retrieved our cars, and began to reassemble our lives. It seemed like it should be easy, nesting together as a full-fledged, engaged couple. Our friends wanted to go out and celebrate our engagement with us. My mom was fully invested in planning our wedding by the time we returned, and my main terrifying task was to find the perfect dress. I wanted to see everyone and revel in their happiness that we were back. But we'd been on the road for eleven months and very quickly I began to realize that re-entry into the real world was not going to be as smooth as I had hoped.

Fred was returning to his job at the same two schools where he had worked before. He knew all of the people and the expectations. I was going to be teaching the entire K–6 school, approximately 280 students, with no assistant. Before we left for Asia, I visited Fred's friend, Ethan, who taught fifth grade for years at this school. I had a great meeting with the principal, and they said they would keep me in mind for my return. When I interviewed on Skype, I knew it would be a big job to teach twice as many grades as I did at Curtis School, but my previous job was filled, I needed to work, and they wanted me. I accepted the position while we were in Laos.

There were many potholes for the start of school. On my first day of orientation at Brawerman, I discovered my entire room was full of books and a piano. There was barely room to walk around. They were renovating the library, and the custodial staff had moved all the contents into my science classroom. In the week before classes started, my supervisor, the assistant to the assistant principal, walked into my classroom and said, "Myself and the rest of the administration don't think you're going to be ready for school next week."

I responded with as much patience as I could muster, "It might help if you could get these books and the piano out of my classroom so I can set up."

Walking to and from work helped immensely in the feeling of being grounded and gave my brain time to prepare for the intense days. Fred wished we were already back on the road. He had two jobs, and he was great with the kids, but he hated the drive to school. It was longer from my condo to his school than he was used to, and he would get frustrated on the way home. I offered to sell the condo or rent it again, saying we could move back to the marina where he had lived, but he repeatedly rejected my suggestions. I was tense about school and wedding planning and figured he was the same. I tried to give him space. He would go in the bedroom, play guitar, and drink away his road rage.

When we first got back, Fred and I had looked at our expenses and made a decision that every other month we would each put five thousand dollars into our joint bank account. The problem was that every time I asked Fred for the money, he would start complaining that we spent too much. I would have to beg him to just write the check. It was my condo and my mortgage, and I'd lived there before he moved in, which meant all the bills were in my name. And it fell to me to make all the payments. I would often say, "Listen, I am happy to talk about our budget and changing it at any time. For the moment, this is our agreement. Please just write the check and give it to me." It was aggravating to have the same conversation all the time. We mainly ate in and still managed to set aside money for future traveling every month. What was he upset about? He just thought Los Angeles was expensive compared to Asia, which it was, but this was where we lived, and we had both lived there before we met.

I liked to cook, and Fred didn't mind shopping and preferred not to cook, so to me, this felt like an equitable sharing of household tasks. I was happy to cook, but over time, I came to realize this was Fred's way of being controlling. He could control how much was spent on food and also continue to control my calories and weight. Sometimes after teaching all day and walking both directions, I was exhausted and just didn't want to cook. Once I ordered Chinese food for dinner, and Fred refused to eat it. He was angry I had spent the money when we had food in the fridge.

When Fred returned from work the next day, he was angrier.

"What's wrong?" I asked him.

"You gave me the bad lunch!"

After cooking dinner, I would usually portion out the leftovers and make our lunches for the next day. I'd always loved taking lunch to school growing up and it was just as easy to make two lunches as one, so I made our lunches every day. I didn't mind. But after Fred threw a fit about the Chinese food, I certainly was not going to send it with him for lunch. We argued about it, but afterward, he admitted he'd complained to a coworker who had said,

"Wait a minute! Someone other than you makes your lunch and you're complaining about what's in your lunch box? If someone was making my lunch, I would never ever complain. I would say thank you very much!" Fred did faithfully tell me the entire story, and it seemed like he did appreciate this perspective, but I felt like I took care of so much and it was never enough.

I knew Fred didn't want me to get fat again, and I worried I would gain back the weight I had lost. I knew that all the walking and hiking and trekking we had done when we were traveling was part of the reason I'd gotten thin. It was two miles from my condo to Brawerman, mainly downhill in the morning but mostly uphill on the way home. I made a commitment to walk to and from school no matter the weather to keep up my physical activity and keep off the weight.

I had always loved having friends over for dinner and hanging out, but these opportunities faded away when Fred moved in. A friend came for dinner one time and Fred was upset there weren't enough leftovers for lunch. I assured him there was plenty of food and options, but I stopped inviting people over as much. I also stopped going to services on Friday nights. Fred had gone with me when we were first dating, but now he said that one temple had music that was too loud, and the other one was too boring. I loved them both, and it was deeply important to me to be involved in my spiritual community. I was torn. I did want to spend time with Fred, but I missed my friends and family. Mostly, I didn't want to fight.

I started calling my mom and friends on my walk home from school. It took about forty minutes to walk home, so I could decompress from my day and chat and get the talking out. I tried to get off the phone before I walked in the door because Fred was often home before I was and he didn't like all the chatting. It seemed like a small thing to be respectful of his wishes, but sometimes I felt left out of my own house. When he moved in, his stuff, which was mostly from his now-deceased parents, took over every empty space in the condo. Where I once had empty space, we now had too many chairs and paintings, as well as many guitars, amps, keyboards, and more.

Once he had a basketball game on in the living room and music playing loudly in our bedroom. I was trying to work on my lesson plans for the next day and had a built-in desk in the kitchen, but I didn't think he needed to occupy both rooms with his music and games. When I said, "I can't work in the kitchen because the basketball game is on loudly in the living room and I can't work in our bedroom because your music is pounding. Can you please turn off one or the other?" He quickly did.

"I didn't notice. You don't have to get so upset."

For our wedding, there were many things to discuss and figure out. One of the first things my mom said to me after Fred and I got off the plane from Mongolia was, "You need a dress." The first time we went dress shopping, I was worried. I thought everything would look terrible on me. My mom and I had an appointment at a fancy store, and I was given a giant dressing room. The staff were very nice, but I was nearly in tears before we started. I was sure that nothing would fit or look decent. I still didn't really comprehend how much weight I'd lost on our trip. I had been at my heaviest on my first date with Fred, and now I weighed less than I had in high school and was trying on dream dresses in Beverly Hills.

It turned out that everything the team brought to me fit, and each one looked better than the one before. Now my mom was crying because I looked beautiful, and I had just been crying because I thought everything would look terrible. At the next place, I went dress shopping with my sister and Teresa. This time, I knew dresses would fit. And while we might not find my exact dress, I looked forward to it because I now knew we would have fun and if there was crying, there would only be happy tears. We also looked for bridesmaids' dresses. That was more challenging. Mainly, things were ugly, but then we went to yet another store and found the perfect dress. It was stunning and we asked, "Does it only come in black?" The woman said that it also came in mulberry, which was the exact pink that matched my pink sapphire ring, so we happily bought that dress in three sizes for three bridesmaids.

I wanted my wedding to not be stressful, but inevitably, with Fred, there were some bumps. We had organized where to have the wedding, who would officiate, and when it would be. Fred would play guitar at the beginning, and he even chose to make beautiful place cards for each guest with photos from our trip, which was a giant project. He was very specific that he wanted to dress formally in a new tuxedo. While he had many ideas about what he wanted, he was highly disinterested in things he didn't care about. He didn't want to go to the brunch the next morning, he didn't want to meet with any of the vendors, and he didn't understand why there had to be so many people. He wouldn't discuss flowers, and he definitely refused to go cake tasting. I kept saying, "Even if our cake tastes terrible and my dress turns purple, at the end of the day we will be married. I want to be married to you forever and the wedding is just one day." I was trying to keep it all in perspective while juggling all the pieces.

My mom and I went to one cake tasting but when they weren't quite ready for us, we looked at their book of ideas. Fred wasn't much of a sweets person, but he did like key lime pie. I fell in love with the idea of mini cupcakes with a small cake for us to cut at the reception because we could have a variety of flavors—including key lime pie. They had chocolate and carrot cake, my favorites. In the end, there were four different cupcake flavors at our wedding. Each guest got two and then the person beside them had the other two. High level cupcake trading took place at our event.

There were also times when Fred seemed to really see me and get me and be the man I wanted to marry. It was his suggestion to ask Joannie Parker, my dear friend and former teacher, to be part of my wedding party along with my sister, Betty and Teresa, two other close friends who were like sisters to me. He surprised me when he asked that *Dodi Li*, which is from the Hebrew, "*Ani L'Dodi V'Dodi Li*" (which translates to "I am my beloved's, and my beloved is mine") be inscribed in Hebrew on the inside of our wedding bands and suggested we each have a small pink sapphire on the inside that only we knew about. I really wanted a special, custom *ketubah*, which is the Jewish wedding contract signed before the wedding. I found a double-ring design and someone who could make it with our names. It was a rainbow of color and flowed with the names. We chose to write our own vows, although most of what I wanted to say was in the ketubah, which I read during the ceremony. I held onto these moments because there were also times when he seemed to get cold feet. He was concerned that marriage would change things, but he did keep saying he wanted to be married to me.

I never thought I would change my name, but both of Fred's parents were deceased and his grandfather had survived the concentration camps. I knew his family name carried a lot of meaning. I wanted him to know how seriously I took our commitment, and I talked to him about changing my name.

"You do not need to change your name."

I said, "I want to add your name to mine. I want you and everyone else to know we are family." I was going to be Lisa Niver Kozel, but the kids at school would call me Mrs. Kozel.

Our wedding took place on December 19, 2009—the first Saturday of winter break at both our schools which meant we could maximize the time we had to travel for our honeymoon. It was almost exactly three years to the day that we'd had our first date, which was January 18, 2007. At our wedding rehearsal, everything really went well. I felt loved and supported by this community of friends and family.

The next morning before our wedding, I could tell something was bothering Fred. I knew he missed his parents, and his friends had been riling him up about how relationships changed after the big day. While getting hair and makeup done with my bridal team, one of the photographers asked me, "Where is Fred?"

"What do you mean?"

Apparently, it was time to take photos of him getting ready and he was nowhere to be found. I called him, feeling frantic. He didn't answer his phone. I started to freak out. Eventually, he called me back. He hadn't heard the phone. He'd gone for a long walk on the beach and was far from our hotel. I said, "Are you coming back?" I wasn't sure if I meant to me, ever, or for this wedding, but I was feeling devastated that I had to yet again be the anchor that pulled him back. Was I always going to have to fight to make him show up? Did he actually want this?

I hung up the phone and burst into tears. The photographers looked at each other. They were a couple and the husband said, "I will take care of Fred. Just give me his number." The wife stayed with me while the husband went to another room to call him. Teresa took my phone and said, "No more calls today."

Betty took me into the bathroom and stood on my feet. She said, "You have been sitting in the makeup chair with your feet off the ground. We have to remind you that you are okay." She never asked me if I wanted to go through with the wedding. I'm not sure what my answer would have been.

We took deep breaths, drank water, ate grapes and cheese, and continued to get dressed. My dress, shoes, and makeup were perfect. I loved my rings and my ketubah, and I hoped Fred wanted to want to work with me to have a meaningful wedding and relationship. I wanted this formal public commitment in front of friends and family. I knew he wanted to marry me but would have been happier with a smaller, simpler ceremony. At last, the photographer poked his head in again to tell me that Fred was back and ready and we were all set to go. I had let go of my fears after my tears dried and believed he just went for that long walk for his own reasons about missing his parents, not about a lack of desire to marry me.

The rest of the day went perfectly. We had photos upstairs at Casa Del Mar by the pool and Fred's face when he first saw me was full of love. The bridal party took photos together and then we had the ketubah signing. It was exactly how I imagined, the feeling of all being together and feeling united as a community. We were on the beach, there was a sunset, we had the best band and great food, but mainly, the people who loved us were all in one place.

We danced together to "Que Sera Sera," a song we heard in Koh Lipe, Thailand, the day we got engaged. When I heard it, I thought, *What will be will be. That is us!*

On Sunday morning, we woke up, had sex, and then needed to get to the brunch. Fred was adamantly refusing to go. I considered going without him. I needed to see my friends and family before they left. Of course, I'd already spent time with them, but I was greedy and wanted to soak up their love.

"What about your aunt and uncle?" I asked him. "They flew here from New York and walked you down the aisle to support you."

Finally, Fred begrudgingly agreed to go next door to where the brunch was being held, but he dragged his feet, making me feel like I had a two-year-old having a temper tantrum chained to my side. This was not what I wanted. I felt angry. He'd agreed to the brunch. He had shared his displeasure in advance, but we had discussed it as a family and now he was making a big ordeal of it again at the last moment. I hated feeling like he was blaming me for making him do something he didn't want to do.

Once we arrived, Fred smiled and talked to people. Did he just have stage fright? Or was this just a set-up so he could blame me for situations he felt insecure about or didn't want to do? I was worried, but I also knew that the weekend and all the planning had left me a bit stressed and exhausted, and he was probably feeling the same.

That evening, my dad drove us to the airport to fly to our honeymoon destination in the Cook Islands. Between us, we had already been many places in the South Pacific, but neither of us had yet been there. Fred had found low-priced tickets, which seemed like a miracle for a December holiday, and had even booked us accommodations in advance, which he never did. We stayed at Areta Beach Villa on Aitutaki first and did a lagoon tour with Teking Tours to the incredible jewel-toned Aitutaki Lagoon. We loved it so much we went twice. We went to small uninhabited islands and took lots of happy photos. Generally, we just enjoyed our time together on the tour, staying late in bed and doing anything we wanted. We also went kayaking, read books in the hammock swings, and saw a local Christmas parade.

While our two-week holiday in paradise felt like a honeymoon initially, a family moved into the villa next to us five days later and their infant cried. The baby woke Fred up and he was pissed. This happened more than once, and Fred complained to the property owners and told the young family they were ruining his honeymoon. He could not seem to get over it. Did I want to be woken up by a baby? No. Babies cry. Fred was furious a baby was near us, but we had only rented our unit and not the entire complex.

Our second stay was on Muri Beach on another island called Rarotonga. Our accommodation wasn't nearly as nice, a simple cottage with not-quite hot water and curtains that almost (but not quite) closed. No babies, though, that was an improvement. Every night after exploring and snorkeling, we found a cheap, happening place to eat with our toes in the sand and watched the sunset with drinks with umbrellas.

At the end of two weeks, we returned to the airport for our long flight back home to Los Angeles. During our stay, we bought some bottles of alcohol we hadn't finished, and Fred brought them to the airport. He was drinking from a plastic bottle so it looked like water, but he was drinking straight vodka. As the day wore on, he got drunker and drunker and jostled the people in line around us. He kept bumping into the man in front of him. I moved in between them, but Fred seemed determined to cause trouble, and I was concerned about him starting a fight. Once we finally got on the plane, I thought we had made it, but Fred was being loud and people were staring. I felt like everyone could see that he was drunk. He was stumbling, he was singing, he was swaying. I was mortified.

Two flight attendants approached us and one of them asked me, "Is he with you?"

I considered my answer but took a deep breath and said, "Yes, unfortunately. We are on our honeymoon."

The second, much younger one, said in the most excited, pre-school-teacher, sing-song voice, "Oh! Congratulations! It's your honeymoon? You must be so excited!"

I looked at her and then back at the first and older flight attendant, who gave me a look of understanding.

"Can you control him?" She asked me in a low voice. He was flinging his seatbelt and nearly hit another passenger. I looked her in the eyes and said, "I am not sure."

I was also not sure that if they made him get off the plane, I would join him—or if I would go home without him and go back to work. Fortunately, soon after, Fred passed out. I had a feeling of dread and was embarrassed by how far down things had slid.

We Said Go Travel

After returning from our honeymoon and settling back into our regular routine, Fred turned his attention to the book he'd always wanted to write about our original journey in Asia. He wanted to call the book *He Said, She Said*, and he thought we should tell the story in alternating pages using our journals. He would write three pages and then send the document to me and I would write three pages. I was excited. I had always wanted to write a book.

As we wrote, I started to research how to promote a book and learned that authors needed a platform. The blogging revolution had happened while we were in Asia. I set out to create a blog for us using the monthly newsletters I'd emailed home to my students. I started with the site Blogger which was part of Google Mail and fit my requirements that it be free, easy to use and I did not need a new password. That year over spring break, we went to Morocco, and while we were sitting in a café in Marrakesh, Fred came up with a name for our new website: We Said Go Travel. I purchased the domain names online and grabbed the handles on social media.

I decided I would commit to writing at least one article a week for our website, and when we returned from Morocco, I posted an article about our adventures that listed where we stayed in Marrakesh and Essaouira, the best foods to try, and some important words to learn. For our overnight adventures by camel into the desert, I did a separate story on Todra Gorge and Ouarzazate. I'd read that authors should also give talks, so I started thinking about where Fred and I could be speakers, who might let us speak, and what our topics would be. I had learned about the Jews of Morocco on our spring break trip, and I decided I would try to give a talk at my temple about the subject. No one else was quite as enthusiastic, including Fred. Ultimately, I convinced the temple to host, and diligently worked on my presentation. I wondered what I'd gotten myself into but figured that, at the very least, my family and friends would want to come and hear me speak.

In between teaching all day and working on my sections of the book at night, I devoted time to networking almost every day. I thought it would be good for the book and the website if I could write travel articles for websites and publications other than ours. I started with Technorati, a site about technology and its impact. The site was new, and I made contact with an editor who offered to publish my stories unpaid, for exposure. He was incredibly patient, sometimes sending articles back to me with edits and suggestions four or five times, but I was determined to learn about online writing. I wrote stories from my experiences including the importance of taking career breaks, how bugs are the new sushi with the story of when I tasted fried crickets in Chiang Mai, and about the Colonial Colombian cities of Santa Marta and Taganga, both north of Cartagena.

When I had a number of articles to link to on our website, I found the courage to reach out to Rob Eshman, the editor-in-chief of the *Jewish Journal*. It's based in Los Angeles and is the largest print circulation magazine for the Jewish community outside of New York City. I knew him because I was a temple hopper, and his wife ran one of the synagogues I attended. I was hopeful Rob might mention my upcoming talk at Stephen Wise Temple about the Moroccan Jews. I figured if you don't ask, you don't get. Rob emailed me back and agreed to mention the talk, then asked if I might be interested in writing a regular travel column for the *Jewish Journal* online. OMG! A regular column! I was elated, but I wrote him back and said I wasn't sure that all my travels were Jewish. Rob said, "It will work out." Soon, more people began approaching me from other websites and publications. Everything I wrote I always linked back to We Said Go Travel.

Throughout all this, Fred mostly sat on the sidelines. While the book was his idea, the website was mine, and it quickly became clear he had very little interest in undertaking the steps that would actually grow it into a business. I continued to post new content every week, but he didn't write unless he was "moved" which was just about never. Similarly, he wanted to have a book that sold, but he was unwilling to work with me to grow our platform. He wasn't impressed that I was speaking at the temple and, in fact, said he wouldn't even be there. I persevered and even hired someone to film the talk for me as I wanted to post it on our website. On the night of the event, Fred did show up and was impressed by how many people were there and how much they liked my presentation. More than forty people attended, making it one of the temple's most successful evening events. I was encouraged and started to think about other places and venues where we could talk to people and share our expertise.

We joined the Los Angeles Consortium of Online Travel (LACOT), a local group that included established bloggers like The Vacation Gals, Johnny Jet, and Dave Levart from Dave's Travel Corner. At every event, I talked to anyone I could to figure out how other people monetized their websites and what plugins or features to add. Fred didn't mind these events and was good at talking to people, much in the same way that he was good at striking up conversations with fellow travelers and getting to know the locals when we were abroad. But afterward, he never followed up on leads and opportunities. I did everything myself but said we were doing it together.

All this time, we continued working on the book, writing our alternating pages, and sending the manuscript back and forth. We had been using our journals, but Fred stopped keeping a journal when we were in Cambodia and Vietnam. That was the part of the trip when my parents had joined us, and he'd complained that our days were too busy and there was too much to write about, so he gave up and never started again. Now that we'd reached the point in the memoir where he no longer had a journal to use, he asked for mine.

Initially, I refused because there was a lot in my journals about how I'd felt during some of the more challenging moments on our trip. But he insisted we couldn't finish the book without it, that he absolutely had to write his share of the pages, and he flatly refused to continue the project unless I gave him access. I relented. I was unwilling to give up the whole endeavor after all the work, plus he had crossed so many boundaries already that this didn't seem that giant. I even hoped that him reading about my feelings might be a catalyst for some helpful conversations. But when I asked him later how he had felt reading about how some of his actions had affected me on our trip, he was dismissive and said, "I just skip over the blah, blah, blah."

I was furious. Now that my deepest feelings had been laid bare, he was choosing to ignore the painful emotions I'd experienced during those eleven months. Unsurprisingly, when he wrote those sections, there was no mention of his bad behavior, or any hint that things weren't always perfect between us. When it was time for edits, he had a very heavy hand, and changed my sections extensively. Sometimes I read my passages which were in italics and while it seemed like I could have written it, it was no longer very true to my emotional experience. There was a lot about how wonderful and amazing Fred was, how lucky I was to have him, and how much incredible sex we had. I rationalized, these things were fundamentally true, so I let them stand.

As I continued making inroads in the travel space, I wrote to the founders of Meet Plan Go, a group dedicated to career breaks, sabbaticals, gap years, and long-term travel. They didn't have a presence in Los Angeles, but one of the founders, Sherry Ott, suggested, "Do you want to host Meet Plan Go in Los Angeles and start the Los Angeles chapter?" We agreed, and our event turned out to be one of the largest for them that year. We had over one hundred people attend. I networked and found all the panelists, including Lisa Napoli, who had just written a book about Bhutan—we donated all our proceeds to the Books to Bhutan Library Project. She introduced me to Richard Bangs, known as the "father of adventure travel" and founder of a rafting and adventure travel company named Mountain Travel Sobek. He agreed to be the keynote speaker, and Jen Leo, the *Los Angeles Times* travel writer, would be our moderator. I worked incredibly hard to find all these people and the turnout and results were hugely gratifying.

Fred was never particularly happy about these successes; sometimes he was even an obstacle. He frequently groused that my efforts for the website took too much time, that there were too many meetings. When I wanted to partner with Hostel International for Meet Plan Go, their coordinator, Tim, agreed to meet with us at the Indian restaurant where I was planning to host the event. We'd never met, but he and I had spent many hours on the phone and corresponding over email. When Tim arrived, he gave me a hug and said he was looking forward to working with us. Fred visibly stiffened when Tim hugged me, and throughout the meeting he was distant and rude. It turned out Fred was upset because he thought I liked Tim.

"Tim is not interested in me," I assured him. "He hugged me because we are friends. And he is gay. Get over it." Fred insisted he didn't want me to hug Tim again. I thought he was going nuts. Maybe he was always nuts. But I had an event to run and I couldn't get sidetracked by his nonsense.

Our platform was growing and We Said Go Travel was gaining traction, but Fred continued to complain about how much time I spent on the website, insisting that the work I was putting in wasn't necessary. He found issues with my other choices as well. Hypercritical, he didn't like clothes with sequins or anything sparkly. I have always loved colors, especially bright ones, but he did not. He was tired of my hula hooping, which he said was lame and not really exercise. Then he claimed to be sensitive to sounds. If I was on the phone or talking to a friend at an event, this disturbed him, but somehow, he loudly practiced his guitar and bass for hours. He would get upset when my hair would start to go gray before I had it colored again, as if I was somehow letting it go gray to intentionally disturb him. He said he only liked what he called "bride hair"—when I had a keratin treatment to make my hair straight. Whenever we traveled and he sat next to me on a plane or bus, he got frustrated because I read too quickly on my Kindle. This baffled me. Kindles are silent. Somehow, Fred noticed when the pages changed, and this annoyed him. I said, "Look at your own device. Don't look at mine. If it bothers you, don't look."

I couldn't understand why Fred was irritable all the time.

After Fred started using my journal to write from, I felt like the last of my truly private spaces in our relationship disappeared. I decided I needed a place that was just for me, so I started a new journal on my computer and called it "Lisa's Journal—NOT for Reading." With all of his furniture, his seven guitars, and his many criticisms about everything, I sometimes felt there wasn't enough space for me even in my own journal.

Despite these ups and downs, I continued to believe that we mainly got along. Fred could still be sweet and supportive, and there was always the allure of the next adventure. When We Said Go Travel had been up and running for nearly a year, Fred decided he really wanted us to go to Taiwan over spring break. I said yes and thought that maybe it was time to film some videos. People at the travel events were all talking about the rise of YouTube and how video was the future of travel journalism. Fred was very encouraging and bought me a used Cisco Flip video camera for fifty dollars on eBay. It had one large red button which turned it on and off, there was no zoom, and the only other moving part was the USB plug which swung out so you could insert it into a computer and copy the footage. It was basic but perfect for me, almost like having an easy-bake oven. We had no clue how the videos would look or sound, but I packed the camera in my bag for Taiwan and off we went.

Taiwan was a marvel for me as a traveler—clean, beautiful, and easy to navigate. The high-speed rail train ran just as you would expect a train to run in a utopian destination, arriving at its location exactly when they said it would, down to the second. We went to Taipei, Tainan, Kenting, and the Penghu Islands, which are generally regarded as the Hawaii of Taiwan. We went to several breathtaking natural destinations, such as Taroko Gorge and Sun Moon Lake. We took videos everywhere we went, and while they were shaky and a bit hard to hear, the little camera was a perfect start. We could still laugh together and enjoy each other's company.

When I returned to school after the break, I mentioned to one of my fifth grade classes, "I have all of these videos from my trip but I don't know how to make a movie."

My student Hannah spoke up, "Hey Mrs. Kozel, I'm going to stay in today at recess and teach you iMovie." It turned out to be the best six-minute tech lesson ever. She told me, "Do this. Press this button," and when I asked about another button she said, "Don't touch that. You don't need that." It was very cut-to-the-chase but enough to get me started making movies for our website.

Sometimes it felt like I was on overload. In addition to improving the website, finishing the book, and traveling with Fred, I was still teaching seven grade levels and writing as much as possible for the *Jewish Journal* and other publications. But I never gave up and even started pitching myself to the media. One day I was invited to be in a local television story for KTLA about career choices, and a camera crew came to my school and filmed me working as a science teacher in the classroom. I knew all of this would help our profile, but it was a lot. I felt like the plate-spinner in the circus.

One weekend, Fred went out of town with his brother. While they were gone, he didn't call or text me at all. I didn't want to be that clingy wife, calling and texting every minute while her spouse is out, so I took a page from his book and decided not to call or text either. I had no idea what time he was coming home on Sunday because he hadn't told me. My parents and I had planned to have dinner together, and I left a note for Fred to tell him where I was going. I left around 4:00 p.m. since my mom and I were planning to choose the wedding photos for our album and I was tired of being home alone.

My parents and I had dinner, and I came back to the condo around 9:30 or 10:00 p.m. The condo was dark. Fred was in our bedroom, asleep. We always got up very early on school days because we had to be at our respective schools between 7:30 and 7:45 a.m. I figured he'd just gone to bed in preparation for the next day.

Fred stirred when I entered our room and, suddenly, he was screaming at me. He called me a whore and screeched out, "Who are you sleeping with?"

I literally could not respond. I had no idea what was going on. He continued to call me names and then demanded, "Where were you?"

As calmly as I could, I stammered, "I had dinner with my parents. I left you a note. Why didn't you call me when you got here? I would have come home. I figured you went to dinner with your brother." My words ran together and my voice trembled as if I had done something wrong. I wondered how much he drank before he stumbled into bed.

He wasn't placated, and his eyes were practically popping out of his head with rage. Shaking and unsure what to do, I turned away, changed my clothes, and got into bed. I lay down facing away from him and stared out into the darkness. Then I heard him turn toward me and he kicked me in the back so hard that I fell off our bed. Sorry, *my* bed. The bed I had bought for graduate school in San Francisco, in the condo I had bought when we first met. I lay on the floor in *my* condo, my back hurting, so startled I could barely breathe. I stood up slowly by the edge of our bed as my clock went flying by my face and cracked against the wall, narrowly missing me. I left the room.

I slipped into the bathroom, locked the door, and stood there thinking. I could leave my condo and go to my parents' house. I had just left there. I could take some clothes and go there and be safe. I had my car. I could drive and I could go. I wasn't sure if that was what I *should* do. I could call someone, but I didn't know who to call or what to say.

Was I in danger? I waited for him to pass out and eventually, exhausted and unable to think about my situation any longer, I went to bed.

The next day, I was a mess. I cried at school, then called and made a therapy appointment on my cell phone in my car because I didn't want anyone to hear me. I left school early and missed a teacher meeting because I couldn't focus. I felt like I was losing my mind. Even my supervisor could see I needed to leave for the day.

I made a plan with my therapist to discuss Fred's behavior with him that evening, and to tell him he must go to therapy with me. When Fred got home, I told him I needed to speak with him. I was very serious and he was concerned. I said, "I don't like what happened last night."

"What happened?"

He claimed to have no memory of the yelling or the throwing or the kicking. I demanded he go to therapy with me, and he acquiesced. We did go for a session a few days later, but when the therapist asked, "Why are you here?" he said, "She made me come here." He never went to therapy again.

I continued going to therapy and convinced myself that *we* were going, but in reality, only I was going, and I was pretty sure I was not the problem. Somehow, I convinced myself that things were getting better. I planned lessons and taught school and worked on the website and looked forward to the next round of travel. If life in Los Angeles wasn't working, there was always another trip on the horizon. I told myself that we were better on the road.

CHAPTER 14

Breaking Up Is Hard to Do

When I finally left Fred after the incident in Chiang Mai, I flew back to Los Angeles alone. I spent most of the flight writing a list of all the things about Fred I didn't like. I wrote pages and pages.

It wasn't that I'd never noticed the things he did; I had just never looked at them collectively or acknowledged a progression. Suddenly his bad behavior on our last day together—when he'd pushed me and I could have broken my neck or my arm and wound up paralyzed or even dead—seemed striking. Maybe when there are so many red flags, I realized, you need to accept that it isn't a parade. Before I left Chiang Mai, I called a therapist I knew. He kept telling me, "You are in danger." But this was hard for me to understand. I was still in shock. Now I was on the plane back to the States without my husband, and I had no roadmap for what lay ahead.

Fred never came back to the United States. I told him in the letter I left at the hotel with his passport that I needed space, and he hardly ever contacted me.

We eventually had a phone call, during which Fred explained to me that he had never hurt anyone. I listened and tried to decide if this meant he thought I had not been hurt, or if I was not someone important enough to count as "anyone." He'd read a book about anger and told me he was ready to see me, he wanted me to come back to Asia, said I could keep track of his behavior and help him. He wanted me to be his kindergarten teacher and give him stickers to help him get his anger under control. He wanted us to go back on the road where I would be alone with him with no support and no one to make sure I was safe. None of this sounded right.

At one point, he emailed me to say he had found us a therapist in Los Angeles: "You can go to his office, and I'll be on Skype." Suddenly, he's willing to go to therapy? I told him he needed to go on his own. These efforts were too little, too late. His anger and his drinking were his problems to solve. I was going to plenty of therapy sessions already.

I lived at my parents' house because my place was still rented, but I wasn't ready to move back to my condo or, honestly, to live alone anyway. But I did need more of my belongings. My sister came to visit from New York City, and she and my mom and I went over to my condo one day to pick up some of my things. It felt terrible to go into the closet and see and touch all of Fred's clothes. When we got back to my parents' house, my sister said, "Isn't this better? Now you have your things." I burst into tears. What I still didn't have, and would never have again, was my husband.

There were many more steps I had to take to untangle our lives. I needed to cancel our joint credit card because Fred was still spending on it, and I was paying the bills. This made me angry. One of the things on the credit card was Fred's health insurance. My attorney Margot said I couldn't cancel the card and put his health insurance at risk. I seethed at the unfairness, but the universe was on my side. Within several days, the bank called me to say there had been fraudulent charges on that card and they had canceled it for me. That settled the issue. I let Margot know so she could tell Fred's lawyer that the card was cancelled and he would need to pay his health insurance with one of his own cards going forward.

As the divorce proceeded, Margot advised that I not have any contact with Fred directly, but he was still in touch with my dad. One day, my dad informed me that I needed to let Fred have the Kindle password. I immediately said no. I had changed it because I was not sharing books with him anymore. My dad patiently explained that I was missing the point. I shouldn't waste my time arguing over ten-dollar books from Amazon, he said, or pay Margot to negotiate over a Kindle. This was not a hill to die on. Ultimately, I did change the password back so Fred could read his Lonely Planet books, but I did it begrudgingly.

A giant battle occurred over digital photos that was dumb and cost me so much money that I still can't think about it without cringing. I remember writing the check to Margot and thinking: This is how people lose their house in a divorce. You fight over something for hours and days and weeks. It honestly makes no difference, but you want to win, and in the end, the only way to pay the enormous bills for all the back and forth is to sell your home.

In this case, Fred wanted access to our Shutterfly photos. I had a Shutterfly account linked to my name and email that I'd had since before we were together, and all the photos we had ever taken on our travels, from the first trip to Fiji to our last days in Thailand, were in this account. I'd used many of the photos for my blog and our website, and thought I might use them for future writing. I didn't want Fred to have access to this account because I worried he might simply go in and delete all the photos out of spite.

I offered to make him a copy of the account linked to a different email. He rejected this idea. Finally, we agreed that I would have Shutterfly put digital copies of all the photos onto DVDs, which I would then send to him. When the DVDs arrived in the mail, they were unlabeled. I had anticipated that each album would be on a separate DVD with a label that said, "Thailand 2012" or "Wedding 2009." But as the DVDs spilled out of the envelope into my lap, it was clear there were no labels—just many, many discs with thousands of photos. I had to laugh. He'd gotten exactly what he asked for, but it was clearly much less useful than a copy of the photos online. I couldn't believe that this particular conflict had created that many billable hours for our attorneys.

When it came time to figure out how to split the website and the business, Fred said he didn't want either. What he did want was half of the rights to our book and half of the money it made. I said no. I wanted the book *and* the website since I had done most of the work on both. My dad again was a voice of reason.

"Fred did write half the book and if you stop working to promote it, it will not sell any copies. Take the website and agree on the book." After several temper tantrums, I acknowledged that he was right. Once our divorce was final, I worked with a different lawyer to create We Said Go Travel LLC with all the right paperwork that said it only belonged to me.

As we worked to disentangle the rest of our finances, Margot told me that Fred was going to owe me money. When I met Fred, he had a mattress on the floor and had been in the Peace Corps, I assumed he was a poor, starving student. But in fact, this was far from the truth. He had inherited money from his family—enough, I reflected later, to steal his ambition, but not enough for him to feel comfortable never working again. Now, thanks to a California state formula, he had to pay me a certain amount of money based on how long we were together and how much money he had. In the beginning, there was drama because the money wasn't arriving in a timely fashion. Eventually, after many calls between the lawyers, he began sending physical checks.

There were times I was angry at Fred for not coming back to Los Angeles and leaving me to sort through the wreckage of our relationship. But he had never been big on taking responsibility, and in some ways, it was easier without him. His refusal to participate or assume any culpability for the demise of our marriage actually made it easier for me to make my decisions. There was no waffling because he wasn't promising to be better, or to do whatever I asked, or showing up at my parents' house in the wee hours of the morning, full of apologies, begging me to take him back. His astonishing lack of sorrow or compassion or effort made me realize my path forward could not include him.

In the fall of 2014, I signed the divorce papers at Margot's office. I didn't expect it to physically hurt so much.

Now that the divorce was final, and since Fred was in still Asia, his brother hired a mover, and through the lawyers, we picked a time for them to pick up his stuff. Soon after, our tenant moved out and I began the process of putting the condo up for sale. I loved my condo, but I knew I could never live there again. I also decided to get rid of my wedding rings. I sold the fourth and final engagement ring with the pink sapphire to my mom's jeweler, who also offered to melt down my wedding band and pay me the value of the gold.

I'd been working with my rabbi on feeling free in all ways from my marriage. I had my lawyer for the legal part, and since I also signed a ketubah, the Jewish wedding contract, I wanted a GET, a Jewish divorce, for support for healing my spirit. I didn't have to get a GET, but I wanted one. Because Fred wasn't coming back, the rabbi said I didn't have to appear in person before the *beit din*, or Jewish religious court. After I was granted my GET, the next step was a *mikveh* or ritual bath.

The rabbi explained that this new mikveh ceremony was not to celebrate my divorce; it was to open the door to the next part of my life. He was about to retire and told me that his nephew had said to him, "You don't have to know everything you are going to do next. You are not writing the whole book; you are simply turning a page to begin the next chapter." I liked this idea. I was moving in a new direction, but I didn't necessarily need to know what lay ahead. Several friends joined me for the ceremony as witnesses, and being in the sacred space and wading in the water reminded me that I was blessed, that I belonged, and that I could forgive myself.

One unexpected thing was how challenging it was to restore my name. I was legally Lisa Niver Kozel but I wanted to go back to Lisa Niver. Banks were simple. They didn't seem to care what name you used, but the airline frequent flyer miles programs were strict. I had to send in copies of my marriage and divorce decrees and practically get the information notarized. But I had my name on every social media account and every website I had ever written for, and there were no tips for updating your online footprint or published content. Every time I found a byline with Kozel, I wrote to the website or publication to get it fixed. This job seemed endless. I'd had no idea when I added Fred's name that the subtraction would feel more like long division married to calculus.

It's Raining Men

In December 2014, a few weeks before my divorce was final, *USA Today* asked me to write a piece for 10Best on the best comedy clubs in Los Angeles. Through a series of misunderstandings, my article was rejected, but the silver lining was that now the editor said instead of being only a Los Angeles expert, I could pitch and write about any destination in the world I wanted. Around this time, my sister's friend Riley, who worked at Ogilvy in New York City, called to ask me a question about fashion. We started to talk about me and what I was doing, and suddenly I was invited to go on my first press trip abroad without Fred.

Ogilvy represented the Irish beer, Guinness, and they were arranging a Guinness Factory press trip to coincide with St. Patrick's Day 2015. The trip would be based in Dublin and mostly about tasting the beer, but she said I could be on their float in the parade. I had never been in a parade, and while I had no idea why they would want a Jewish American journalist from Los Angeles to be on their float, I was ecstatic. I started buying green clothes to look as much like a leprechaun as possible.

This press trip to Ireland would be my first international travel with my passport restored to my original name, which was a huge deal to me. Additionally, Fred and I had fought about going to Ireland. He said it would be too expensive and out of our budget. Now, I was invited to go to one of my dream destinations and it was costing me nothing.

On my first day there, Riley and I explored Dublin, and the contrast with Los Angeles struck me. Every narrow street and stone building seemed to seep with history. I'd read about the forty shades of green in Ireland, but I hadn't thought about how the feeling of a historic city would remind me of being in other ancient places, like Jerusalem. When we had a whiskey tasting in my hotel bar at the Brooks Hotel, they explained about the peat and the smoke and the different flavors and I realized—I really do not like whiskey.

The following day, I joined my journalist group for a tour of the Guinness factory, which was my first brewery tour. I didn't drink a lot of beer but did like dark beers like Boddingtons. During lunch on the property, where nearly everything was cooked or baked with beer, including the tasty bread and superb chocolate mousse, I asked permission to invite Scott, my flight seatmate. I knew he was still in Dublin, loved Guinness, and we had space on our tour. Thank goodness he joined us, as unlike me or Chris—the other journalist in my group—he was a Guinness aficionado. Scott had the most thoughtful and appropriate questions about beer. There were also constant samples. Scott drank his and most of mine, saying, "You cannot waste this excellent beer!" whenever I tried to put something down unfinished. When we stopped to wait our turn to learn to pour the perfect pint, he turned to me and said, "I hope I'm not asking too many questions."

I said, "You are saving our day!"

Chris asked him, "How do you know Lisa?"

Scott replied, "I slept with her on the way over!" We all laughed, and I realized with delight that I was on tour with several handsome men, and I was in Ireland. I could see that things could only get better. However, I had no idea how much they were going to improve right away.

That night, I met the rest of our group at the Bea Beata Festival Dinner for St. Patrick's Day Weekend, held at the Guinness Storehouse. Amid the decorative fairy lights and creative concoctions made with Guinness, I met the three journalists joining us from a popular men's lifestyle website in Canada and was immediately drawn to the one who was tall, dark, handsome, and Jewish. Their flight was delayed causing them to miss the first tour with us at the brewery. I was seated next to him and loved how he leaned in to whisper in my ear. He made an effort to get me the rolls or wine I preferred and draped his arm over the back of my chair. He was charming and I enjoyed having a man's attention.

Since the divorce had been finalized, and even once or twice in the months before I was officially single, I had very, very slowly begun to dip my toe back into the world of dating. This wasn't always intentional, and these encounters were often weird because my head and my heart were still all over the place.

Now, I was sitting next to hot Andrew from Toronto at the special event Bea Beata Festival Dinner at the Guinness Storehouse in Ireland. I was enjoying his attention and our dinner. After the meal, our group went to Grogan's Pub on the corner of Williams Street and Coppinger, next to our hotel.

I anticipated that Andrew would keep talking to me, but he sat at the bar with two young women who were already there ingratiating himself immediately. I had a drink with the rest of our group and then said I was going back to the hotel. Chris offered to walk me home, which was really his excuse to leave since we were literally half a block from the entrance to our hotel. As we headed toward the door, Andrew leaned back from his seat between the two women and asked, "You're leaving?"

I said, "Goodnight," and kept walking.

The next day was busy with touring and soaking up Irish culture. Together, we went to St. Stephen's Garden, The Little Museum, and Guinness PopUp History, and that night had another long sumptuous dinner and went to another local hangout for more drinks. Andrew and his two friends were chatting and drinking in another part of the bar. As I walked by, Andrew grabbed my arm and hugged me close to him and said, "Last night you left without saying good-bye."

"Last night, you left me to talk to those women at the bar."

"Tell me your room number and I'll come by after I finish my drink."

I told him, because I was positive he wouldn't show up. He was just a flirt.

I went back to the hotel and fell asleep quickly. Then I heard noises. Who was knocking on my door? What time was it? Where was I? I put on a robe and walked to the door and to my complete shock, there was Andrew.

"I told you I would come by."

I stared at him. "I didn't believe you."

He pushed me back toward the wall, started kissing me, and said, "You're wearing a robe."

"I was sleeping."

He smiled and said, "Not anymore."

As he moved us toward the bed and moved his hands expertly down my body, I wondered where someone learned skills like this. It felt incredible. I had left Ireland and arrived in heaven and I felt so in the moment. I wasn't worried about anything or what anyone thought about Fred or any mistakes in my marriage or judgment. I just felt happy and free and content.

Not wanting to be outdone, it was my turn to please him, and, boy, was he surprised. Andrew and I were up for hours and hours before I had to give in to the jet lag and passed out.

The following morning, our group joined a bus tour with other international journalists for a day trip to Wicklow, located thirty miles outside Dublin. I sat on the bus with Andrew and we chatted. I walked on nature trails with the forty shades of green of the Irish countryside in my all-green attire. Between each site, I snuggled on my seat with him and got a bit too lost in remembering how nice it was to travel with someone. But after lunch, it felt quite cold on the bus. It seemed Andrew was no longer speaking to me and sat as far as he could from me in the seat, talking with everyone on the bus but me.

I felt a bit bereft and near tears as I ran back to my room when we reached the hotel. I was working so hard to build a new life and meeting Andrew reminded me of how lonely I had been feeling.

Exhausted from the all-night antics, nearly delirious from jet lag, and drained from the internal and external journeys, I got in the shower, started to wash my hair, and heard insistent pounding on my door. I put a towel around myself, shampoo suds practically going up to the ceiling, and called out, "Who is it?"

Andrew, on the other side, yelled, "Open the door."

"I'm in the shower."

"You're not in the shower anymore."

"Why are you pounding on my door?" I said back. "You didn't want to be near me or talk to me on the bus."

"Why were you acting so clingy?"

I burst into tears. I blabbered about how it just felt nice to be near someone again and I was rebuilding my travel life but sometimes it was just hard. Andrew held me and said, "I thought you were more upset about your divorce than you let on."

This new chapter in my life included a rollercoaster of feelings. I didn't doubt that I'd needed to leave my marriage, but I was still mourning the loss of what it could have been if Fred had been the man I imagined he always was. I tried to shake my head and stay in the present. I was in Ireland, back in bed with a hot, naked man.

The entire country seemed to be arriving in Dublin for the massive St. Patrick's Day Parade. The international journalists were all invited to ride on a double-decker bus with Guinness. On the morning of the parade, the exhaustion and uncertainty were ringing in my ears. I started questioning why they had invited me. Who was I to be in an international parade? And all of a sudden, I couldn't catch my breath. I grabbed the press coordinator's hand and he saw the look in my eyes and called out for Andrew to come over to me. Andrew grabbed my arm and took me outside the building. It was too warm in the waiting area, and I had all my layers on.

He said, "Just look in my eyes. Try to breathe with me." He helped me take off the coat and hat and scarf that were overheating me and got me water. He told me it feels terrible, but it is only a panic attack. I cried and then was able to dry my tears, accept his hug, and get on the damn bus for the parade. Once I got upstairs and outside, on the second level of the bus, and needed all my warm green leprechaun gear, I quickly got into the mood of celebration. I loved being in the parade.

When I returned to the States, Richard Bangs called and invited me to be the host of a second Orbitz web series in Bermuda. The Orbitz team had seen my zipline video from Puerto Rico and thought I was funny and would be an engaging host for the Proper Fun segments, which would highlight the best of British Bermuda. For my first visit, I walked on the pink sand beaches, shopped in the quaint town, and drank the local libation: the Dark and Stormy. It wasn't that long since we'd filmed together, but I felt like a completely different person. I felt confident and capable.

While we were filming in a cave, the director took a great, sexy photo of me in silhouette. It astonished me how good I looked. Apparently, the local guide I was interviewing about adventure in Bermuda, who jumped from a cliff for our video, was entranced. He followed me on Facebook and messaged me immediately after our session wrapped. We quickly switched from Facebook messenger to the local cellphone I had from the team, and as the day wore on, our text messages shifted to a plan for after-dinner drinks and the hot tub. But when we rendezvoused that night, we never left my room. Turns out my skills worked on all islands and male companions. We tried meeting up again, but my schedule was packed, and we couldn't make it happen. On my first Orbitz trip to Puerto Rico, I had cried myself to sleep at night, but on this trip, there was passion and joy. I was still in turmoil from all the changes in my life, but on this trip, I had successfully compartmentalized these feelings so they didn't interfere with my romantic moments.

My trysts in Ireland and Bermuda were light and breezy, and they reminded me of my days working on cruise ships. However, a short time later on a trip to St. Kitts, I felt like I was starting to cross the line. The man seated next to me on the plane from Miami also happened to be staying at the same hotel for work, and after we chatted on the flight, I left a note at the front desk and he called me in my room. After dinner, we went swimming and he brought drinks. I took him back to my room and had sex with him. But this time it didn't feel right, and I knew this was a habit I needed to break. I had no idea who he was. It was starting to feel reckless.

My schedule started filling up with more offers and I was able to select ones that fed my soul. From a group trip in Hamburg, Germany, I hopped a short flight to Genoa, Italy, to see friends before meeting my next group in Israel. I arrived several days before the other journalists, and while most of this first leg on my own went very well, there were a few moments when my courage faltered. When I arrived at The Ritz–Carlton Herzliya, they handed me my room key in a large white envelope. When I turned it over, there was a stunning photo of me as a bride to personalize my stay. I knew they had searched online to find a photo of me, and while it was an exceptionally beautiful picture of me, I was dismayed. Seeing myself so happy on that day was an awkward reminder of where I had been and where I was now. I'd wanted to be in Israel with Fred at some point, but now I was finally here, at one of the most expensive hotels no less, and I felt sucker punched. I kept my composure, thanked them, and then went to my giant room where I sat down on the bed, took some deep breaths, and thought about how I had taken care of myself. When my marriage was broken, I left. I had picked myself back up and figured out how to travel again. I was in Israel.

There were other times along the way where I struggled to accept the gifts of my hard efforts. People were helping me grow bigger and get better bylines. At times I was jealous of the people I met who *only* did photos or articles or video or social media, but it seemed like the right choice to work hard at all of them and see what could happen. Each trip was better than the one before.

The next invitation that came my way was for a cruise on Viking Atla, a river cruise, which I had never done. It went from Budapest to Nuremberg on the water at Christmastime, which I strongly suspected would be freezing. I insisted that the Viking PR team fly me with a two-night stop in New York City so I could raid my sister's closet for a proper winter coat and other necessary items for this adventure. When I arrived at the ship, I discovered I was nearly the only one in our group who had come without a plus one. This was disappointing, but in truth, I wasn't sure who I could have brought with me. Most people I knew had holiday plans. As we set out, I worried it would be more of a challenge to fit in with this group. This was my first press trip with what seemed like endless happy couples. It felt awkward. Many of the journalists I traveled with were part of a couple, but when we were all there solo, we spent the days together. This trip was clearly going to be different.

Eventually, I settled into the trip and made friends, and before long, two of the journalists, Carolann and Macrae from One Modern Couple, took me under their wing and always made sure I had a place to eat among the sea of people with a plus one.

The group of journalists Viking had brought together turned out to be a talented bunch, and people shared their best practices concerning video, social media, and writing. I was committed to improving all my skills, and the cruise was a great opportunity to see how some very successful people in my industry used travel to make money. I learned about Twitter chats and participated in one for the first time. I filmed video constantly and ultimately made more than thirty short videos about the trip. For Chanukah, Shabbat, and my dad's birthday on Friday, December 11, I explored what was the oldest Jewish Community in Southern Germany in Regensburg. Though it was cold, blustery, and sometimes raining, I went on a ship's walking tour every day in every port. I made a connection to write two articles about the trip for Cruiseline. com and was quite proud of myself for not sleeping with anyone on the trip.

Through the same friend at Ogilvy who had put me forward for the Ireland trip, I was invited to be part of a project with American Express. I could choose any domestic destination I wanted, and they would give me Starpoints to book the hotel and reimburse me for our flights and restaurants so I could promote the benefits of using their credit card. It was very exciting. This time, I invited Teresa as my plus-one, and she picked New Orleans as our destination. She wanted to go somewhere neither of us had been. I took care of the travel logistics, and she picked out all the James Beard award-winning restaurants where we would eat.

When her flight from Philadelphia was delayed by weather, I ended up alone in the city for the first night. As I wandered in the French Quarter with its distinctive southern balconies covered in flowers and jazz music spilling out from bars and cafés, on North Peters Street, I found myself in front of the famed Coyote Ugly Saloon, the notorious place known for women dancing on bars. It was loud, like Mardi Gras was starting months early. I went inside, squeezing my way through the crowd. I asked one of the women if I could hula hoop too. She said, "As long as you get up on this bar, you can do whatever you want!" I climbed right up and she handed me one hoop and then another. I had a great time dancing with her and felt powerful.

Teresa and I spent the next few days exploring the city and eating great meals. While we were there, I matched on Hinge with Benjamin, a bona fide traveler who worked for the Travel Channel and the Discovery Channel. We chatted online extensively and made plans to meet up when I returned to LA.

Benjamin was charming and extremely kind. We both lived to travel and loved to explore new places above and under water. He was also newly and nearly out of his marriage. His situation was complicated, and he was supportive and understanding of mine. He said that happy couples don't get divorced. He connected with me on important issues. I really liked him. He was encouraging about my videos, which he said he would watch, and then actually did. He had filmed, directed, and produced shows all over the world.

At one point, I'd been hired to do a video project for a new sunscreen brand, but it wasn't working, and I wasn't happy with it. Benjamin offered to watch it with me. He said afterward, "I understand why you don't like it. It's not as good as your other videos." This stung a bit, but I agreed with him. Then he said, "Here is how I would fix it." He suggested I be on camera holding the product with the beach in the background while explaining why it was better, then go to B-roll shots.

While I liked his idea, I said, "But there's no way for me to film that."

To which he replied, "Lisa, I'm going to help you. I will film it. We can do it together." I was astonished by his thoughtfulness and generosity. Being supportive seemed to be his natural state. When he asked me why I had left my marriage, I was embarrassed to tell him the story, but he said, "Let me tell you my story first. Then you'll see that yours can't be worse." He had nice friends and was always kind and positive. I did really like him, but he traveled often for work and had young kids with his ex, so it didn't work out for us to be together. I wanted someone who had more time and could travel with me; that wasn't in the cards with Benjamin. Still, it felt enormously different from Fred and the others I had been with since. I could see progress.

Project Restart

It was becoming clear that continuing to travel was possible, but I wondered if I could support myself this way. I knew I shouldn't compare my potential earnings as a travel blogger to what I would have made if I stayed in medical school. I had left that path long ago and always felt good about that choice. The website, which had provided a small but steady stream of income while we were traveling, could not support my living expenses in a city. Could I make a living doing this? I wanted to find out if anyone, even the more experienced writers, were making a living this way.

I knew I could go back to teaching and make decent money. I still loved teaching and working with kids, but I didn't always love how I was treated as a teacher.

As a science teacher, I had often gone to conferences and workshops to meet and learn from other science educators about what was new in our field of teaching and what had been successful in their classrooms. I figured there must be similar places where journalists could go to learn together. I decided that for the next year, I would go to every conference I could to see what I could learn about how to build a legitimate career—and make money—as a travel writer. It was one thing for all these companies and destinations to offer me fabulous places to stay and review, but I also needed to be able to generate a salary. I wasn't sure how willing the more experienced journalists would be to share their secrets. If people *were* making money, I wondered if they'd be honest about it.

I started with the Los Angeles Travel and Adventure Show, a consumer show for people to learn about destinations. From Aruba and Antarctica to Zambia, this was an entire convention center full of exotic, fascinating places to go. I passed out my business card and dreamed of where I could go next, and even spoke with Patricia Schultz, author of 1000 *Places to See Before You Die*. I felt like I was meeting the right people and finding opportunities, but I still wasn't convinced travel could be a full-time job.

My next conference was a relatively new one in Bloomington, Minnesota, called the Travel Bloggers Exchange, or TBEX. Many of my blogging and traveling friends had been in past years, and it was reputed to be one large party. I wasn't sure how much learning there would be, but I was able to work out a deal with the new Hyatt Regency Bloomington to comp my stay, so I figured, why not? I had much more free time now that I wasn't wavering and placating Fred. I sometimes wished for someone to share experiences with, but being solo was a huge improvement overall. I was ready to squeeze every drop of knowledge out of the scheduled sessions and networking lounges. *Maybe this can work out.*

Next, I went to a few local conferences, no flying required. I drove to Long Beach for the Scuba Show, the largest consumer diving show in the world. There were hundreds of vendors grouped by parts of the globe. The aisles were packed with divers looking for their next underwater adventure. The minute I walked in the door, I was overwhelmed because I wanted to go absolutely everywhere. As I left, I called Teresa and told her that I nearly wanted to lay down on the floor and cry. I wanted to dive in all of these places.

She said, "For tomorrow, find the five places you most want to go in the next year and focus on those."

If I could find a way to get paid for diving all over the world, that would be the holy grail.

Each conference gave me more information. I was improving but searching for benchmarks. When you make up your own career, how do you know if you're really making progress or when it's time to give up? The other bloggers and writers I knew told me they were not getting offered the trips or as many opportunities as I was. Did this mean I was a success? Should I be proud of myself yet?

Dave from Dave's Travel Corner and I had talked about creating a Global Travel Influencers group, in order to get more trips, make more money, and pair journalists with assignments. It had a lot of potential, but everyone was traveling and busy and we needed someone to actually run the group. None of us wanted to be the one to stay home. Through this group, I learned about the conference Travel Media Showcase, a place for vetted content creators to meet with destinations and plan future trips.

Prior to the start of the Travel Media Showcase in Texas, I met Tammillee Tillison of Tammillee's Tips, one of the bloggers also invited on the pre-conference girlfriend getaway weekend in Grapevine, Texas. She was rapidly finishing a challenge to do forty new things before her fortieth birthday, which we would celebrate the next week during the conference. I fell in love with this concept and kept asking her questions about her forty things. I couldn't imagine finding that many and actually doing them. A few of the other women suggested I also could do a 40 Before 40 challenge, to which I quickly replied, "No, I can't."

"Of course, you can!" they all chorused.

"No, I really can't." This went on for several bus rides, meals, and other activities until finally, one of the women, Kelly, looked at me and said, "Wait...can you not do it because you're over forty?"

"Yep!"

The idea of doing "50 Things Before 50" stayed with me throughout the conference, and I started testing out the concept with the new people I met. During meetings, if a PR team offered me a trip to Montana about craft beer, or a food festival in Canada, I would say, "I'm starting a new project where I do fifty adventures before I turn fifty, and I'm looking for new challenges. What ideas do you have?" To my amazement, they all loved it, and every PR team was full of suggestions. I could go on a rattlesnake round-up in Lubbock, Texas, I could shoot a cannon, stay at a scary fort, and even go to a bordello and dress like a madame. I could fly in a B-1 bomber and ride a longhorn. These story ideas brought a whole new world of possibilities. Suddenly, this 50 Things idea seemed possible. Maybe turning fifty could be a celebration.

I started my official list accidentally a few days later when I returned from the TMS conference and went to lunch with Ronit, a friend from high school.

While I was explaining the 50 Things concept, Ronit said, "Start now."

"Start what now?" I asked.

"Let me help you order sushi."

I stared at her. It took me a long time to even try pizza, a staple food for most children, because of bad experiences with other foods, like strawberries, which made my lips swell up. She knew I was a picky eater, afraid to try new things because of my previous allergic reactions.

"Maybe you'll like it, but even if you don't, it can be on your list." She knew about my food allergies and was insistent this would be okay.

We looked at the menu, and Ronit recommended salmon sashimi with avocado as an excellent choice. I didn't think it sounded excellent at all.

When it arrived, I stared at the small, slimy orange mound of raw fish hiding beneath the green avocado, thinking this was a terrible idea. But I had agreed, I picked up the chopsticks and put it in my mouth. It wasn't the worst thing I'd ever eaten but I knew I would never order it again.

It was a very small step, but Ronit was encouraging. I wrote it down on a new list that I made on my phone. In the days that followed, I wondered if I was actually doing fifty challenges, and if this even really counted as one of them. The past few years had shown me that small steps could add up to big changes. Mainly I felt comforted by my ability to quit the project at any time. I told everyone I was considering doing 50 Things Before 50, but I just might not.

A few days later at the pool near my house, where I went to swim laps, the water felt chilly, and I remembered that someone had recently recommended sitting in the hot tub to warm up before going in the cooler waters. Honestly, I thought it sounded like a completely stupid idea but I'd committed to considering doing new things, so I decided I could step in the hot tub first. After swimming and diving all over the world, including dry suit diving in Juneau, Alaska, I figured who cares if the water is cold. Hot tubs had very little appeal to me, but if you say you are going to try new things, you have to start somewhere.

I stepped into the hot tub and immediately remembered why I've never much liked hot tubs. They feel too hot. I stayed for a few minutes, then walked over to the pool to swim. The contrast of temperatures from the hot tub to the pool felt more aggravating to me than the cold had originally. I decided I wouldn't do that again, but I had considered someone else's suggestion and made progress on my list of challenges. Just because other people think it's a good idea doesn't mean it's right for me.

I thought back on all the times when I was forced to consider Fred's opinion when he insisted that he knew best, and I knew he was wrong, but I acquiesced to keep the peace. Now, I could simply dismiss things that didn't work for me with no debate, arguing, or consequences. I could put my own ideas first, I could listen to other people's ideas, and then pick what worked for me. *I am starting very small, which is okay, and for me, a perfect way to start.*

50 New Things Before 50

1. Trying sushi
2. Going in the hot tub before the pool

Upping Your Game

After my whirlwind of travel conferences, I knew I wasn't giving up. At least, I wasn't giving up, *yet*. I constantly reserved the right to give up at any point. I still felt that I needed to be very responsible about the choices I was making, because I'd been through so much to get to where I was now and didn't want to squander my fresh start. I still had to remind myself that I had started over again many times, and regardless of whether I'd ended up doing what I'd originally imagined or flying on a trapeze at Club Med, it had always worked out. I had done it many times long before I met Fred, and now that I would hopefully have a long life without him, I could do it again.

From talking to people at Travel Media Showcase, it seemed like video might be a way I could differentiate as a travel journalist. I'd gotten comfortable filming and editing with my little, ultra-basic Flip. For my next adventure, I would be scuba diving when I visited my friend on her cruise ship, and I wanted to be able to film underwater. I didn't want to spend a lot of money on a camera and was not in a place to get sponsored by GoPro, the most expensive and well-known underwater camera currently available. But I also didn't have much experience purchasing technology. Incredibly, I had never bought electronics or even ordered anything online when I was with Fred.

I ran a website. I could figure this out.

I knew from traveling long-term that, sooner or later, everything gets broken. My laptop. My camera. My hard drive. The Kindle. Every single thing had broken at some point. Some were dropped, some had electronics issues, some had adaptor problems. I had never lost anything simply by forgetting it, but the road, the sand, the sun, and the power differences had, at some point, caused every device to succumb. I knew from experience that backing up something once didn't count because you could easily lose the whole drive dropping it out of your backpack on the bus ride from Chennai to Pondicherry.

Given that everything eventually got lost or broken, I didn't want to spend five hundred dollars on an underwater video camera I wasn't even sure I would be able to use. I started to Google rental cameras. Maybe it would make sense to rent a camera and underwater housing (the case that keeps the camera from getting wet and ruined). I kept pondering and stumbled upon GoPro clones on Amazon. The cameras looked like GoPros, came with the underwater housing, and only cost $49.99. This seemed doable. The reviews were decent. I took a deep breath and added it to my cart.

Of course, now I would need my first underwater selfie stick to film with my new camera. I had a brief freakout thinking about all the things I would need to bring with me: phone, backup phone, underwater camera, microphone, selfie stick, external hard drive, laptop, extra chargers, cables, and my dive computer and its charger, which is my most important piece of safety equipment. The dive computer tracks depth and time underwater and applies that information to track the dissolved nitrogen in my body during a dive. It tells me how much dive time is left at a certain depth and, most importantly, beeps if I am ascending too quickly. It's a depth gauge and timer, and I will not dive without one. Some people dive with two, in case the battery on the first one runs out. I told myself that one more selfie stick would not break the proverbial camel's back, but it was starting to seem like I might need bigger luggage.

As I searched for an underwater selfie stick, I happened upon a giant green one. I've always loved green ever since I was a little girl. My mom once told me, "I knew it was your favorite color because that crayon was always the shortest." Now I wondered, *Will this selfie stick change my life? If it improves it, does it count as one of my fifty things? I love green, I love diving. Other people use selfie sticks. I can make this happen.*

A few days later, the new video camera arrived, along with a few other items I'd purchased for the trip, including an SD memory card to store all the photos and videos. I felt like I had everything I needed. Then I realized I had to format the card. There was no Fred to do it for me. But I didn't call anyone—I simply sat down and slowly and carefully read the instructions all on my own. *I am smart*, I kept reminding myself. *I am smart. I can do things myself.* Fred was often unsupportive of my talents, and I let him have control of so many things for so long.

Not only did I figure out the card, but I also put together the camera wrist mount that I could use instead of the selfie stick. After all my hours of eye exercises, I needed to think about how the parts fit together. I stopped. I took deep breaths and looked at the instructions again. I searched for the parts I needed and channeled my elementary school students, who were always perfectly happy to just keep trying as long as I had a smile on my face and told them they could do it. Eventually, I got the wrist mount to work, and when I did, I thought, *I will never, ever take this apart because I do not want to have to figure it out again.* At last, everything was assembled, and I was ready to be a real underwater videographer.

I decided to think about my small successes and attempt to do things with much less drama. I had been perseverating about going to the Travel Classics Conference in Phoenix in November. There were many permutations of airports, prices, and flight times. I imagined myself ordering the video camera and putting it together. I could do this! I didn't have to do it perfectly, I just needed to buy the ticket. Which I did.

3. Buy a new video camera
4. Buy the bright GREEN selfie stick
5. Assemble the wrist mount all on my own
6. Buy tickets to Travel Classics—making your own decisions

Back on the Water

In June 2016, my friend Zoey, who was my very first ship room-mate, suggested I sail with her as her guest on her current ship, *Carnival Breeze*, one of Carnival Cruises' ships. When I first started working cruises, she'd generally looked out for me. Even though I'd spent hundreds of weeks working on over a dozen different ships, I'd never traveled on Carnival. But they were known as the "fun" ships and Zoey was full of life, I decided this would be my next trip.

As part of my evolution as a businessperson, I took my new knowledge from my winter trip on Viking Atla, the Christmas market cruise from Budapest to Nuremberg, with all I had learned about Twitter chats to the bank. These Twitter chats happened regularly and often happened on #TravelTuesday. Some were hosted by travel experts and some by travel brands, especially the Expedia or Orbitz clones trying to gain more market share.

I had been approached to host one. The brand, in this case One Travel, hires a person they think can bring in more followers to lead their one-hour chat on Twitter. The host asks pre-selected questions every five to ten minutes, or whatever the agreed-upon set interview is, and engages with the people participating. I agreed to be the paid host before I left on the next cruise and would take photos and videos from the Caribbean to talk about all the places we were stopping for the next one. I prepared my answers in the site, TweetDeck, which was where you could schedule tweets in advance and add photos as well as links to videos and articles. I was going to be paid $250 for each one, a decent going rate at that time. One Travel approached me, and we talked about if I could go on one of the trips that *they* sold to do more videos for them. They hoped to raise their online engagement and brand awareness by producing chats with travel experts. We could track how it was going by using hashtags in the social media posts. I used several hashtag tracking tools to keep track of how well we were doing, like Talkwalker, Hashtagify, and TweetReach.

Many of my travel friends had also hosted chats with them. The host can encourage audiences to tweet questions and often there's a trip giveaway or some other prize. It felt like a bit of madness trying to keep up with all the incoming tweets and respond to them to encourage further discussion, but I definitely was adding "mastering Twitter chats" to my list of fifty things.

For my first chat on the Viking Atla cruise, I sat next to Simon and Ramsey and watched what they did, and Carolann taught me about the scheduling app, TweetDeck. After their help, I knew how my chat should work. I just had to take the time and go slowly through the steps to set up my own.

I searched through several past chats from the brand and made suggestions for what we could ask for mine. I worked diligently on every step. Their PR person and I exchanged several emails, and after the questions were set, I worked on my answers.

I could set up my questions and answers to automatically populate on Twitter during the chat using TweetDeck so I could focus on engaging with people. You load the tweets and, like magic, they appear at the right time.

On the day of the first chat, I was overly prepared, though a bit nervous that even though I had set it all up and tested it, it wouldn't work properly. Each part of every tweet had to be correct in the scheduling app. The time, the date, the hashtags. It needed to be very precise. Both the brand and I had sent out tweets in advance of the chat for several days, inviting people to join us. There were often travel chats on Tuesdays. People knew when to show up. I had also done an article on my site promoting that we would be having a chat to talk about Italy and my trip with Insight Vacations Luxury Gold. But, even with all my preparation, I wasn't confident I knew what I was doing. I was nervous something would go wrong.

I had practiced, figured it out, learned the steps...and it turned out to be a giant success! There was tremendous engagement. The brand was so happy! We had a larger than expected turnout. I had invited everyone I knew, and I kept the chat going. People loved my photos and my videos. There was a way to count how many tweets were being sent and what the engagement was on the main hashtag. I knew what it had been for past chats and this day was much higher. I felt confident about my newfound skills and planned to do another Twitter chat about my adventures with Zoey in the Caribbean, which would be full of opportunities for my 50 Things list.

Although my cruise with Zoey departed from Galveston, Texas, I flew to Houston with my brand-new underwater video camera and selfie stick and all my other equipment in my luggage and ready to go. Of course, I was flying in prior to the ship embarkation so I wouldn't miss it if there were any delays. On my way to my hotel, I had a minor freakout because I realized I hadn't accurately assessed the travel time between the airport and the ship. I studied the timing of my return flight and realized it wasn't going to work and that I would have to buy another return ticket. Taking a deep breath, I reminded myself this wasn't the end of the world. From now on, I decided, the only "F" word I was going to use during travel was "flexible."

The morning my cruise started, I got organized at my hotel and took a prearranged taxi to the pier. Zoey and I grabbed a bite at her favorite breakfast spot a couple blocks from our pier, and then she brought my luggage onboard through the crew gangway while I stood in line to process my passport, registration, and get my ship card, which would allow me access to the ship. I would be staying in her cabin while she stayed in her boyfriend's much larger officer's cabin, so I would have access to the crew areas. She had to work, and after checking in, I wandered around the ship, learning everything I could about this vessel. I was glad I'd accepted this gift to travel with her.

Zoey's office was closed for sail-away, which is when the ship leaves the pier. There was a party onboard to celebrate the beginning of the cruise. On Princess Cruises, they play the theme from the show *The Love Boat*, but on Carnival it was an all-out jam session with a live band. Carnival Cruises had a partnership with Dr. Seuss, which meant that you could have photos with Sam I Am, Thing 1 and Thing 2! The cruise staff all wore red shirts and black shorts, pumping up the crowd and leading line dancing by the pool. I rushed over to join in.

Zoey laughed and said, "You were born to be on the entertainment team!" We leaned against the ship's railing and took photos as we left the port.

Before Zoey needed to go back to her Port and Shopping desk to answer guest questions, we made a plan to meet at 6:30 p.m. for dinner. Meanwhile, I continued my ship explorations, and on the very top deck, I discovered the Sky Course. It's a ropes course with a sea breeze and view of the ocean, towering above the ship. There were colorful ropes and ladders and I figured they strap people in, but it looked insane. Who would do this?

I approached the two guys running the course, and they said it was always busy except for now on the first night because people were busy getting settled in. He asked if I had shorts on under my dress which I did not. I contemplated the idea. It really would be good for my list. "Why don't you go get shorts right now before you talk yourself out of going."

I looked at him and smiled. "I will be right back."

He said, "We will be right here." *He is really cute.*

I ran to Zoey's cabin ten decks below, changed into shorts, grabbed my phone for photo evidence, and rushed back to the course before it got busy—but mainly before I could decide it was too scary for me to even attempt. I kept thinking about *American Ninja Warrior*, the television show, which I happened to love. This course wasn't as hard or as big as the one on TV, which had balance obstacles and you had to perform lachés (jumps across) six feet with no ropes and then run up the fourteen-foot warped wall, but it was high. I would be in a harness over the mini-golf course below, looking out over the open ocean high above the ship. I arrived back on the top deck feeling somewhat terrified and energized at the same time.

Before I could think too much about what was going to happen, one of the guys strapped me in. I handed him my phone and asked for photo evidence, then looked out over the skinny bridge, a series of bright blue steps separated by blue rope and just enough space from one to the next. In the distance was a bright yellow platform, I started making my way, carefully inching one step at a time. There were ropes you could hold on to, and I did. I could feel my heart jumping out of my chest. This was safe. I could do it. I moved toward the post to turn to the next obstacle.

At one point, I started to freak out and thought I might hyperventilate when I had to travel by moving my feet side to side along a rope. I wanted to hang on the straps that were keeping me safe, but the hot men encouraged me to lift my hands out to my sides up in the air like a tightrope walker. I didn't think I could continue, but there was a nine-year-old-boy behind me, and he couldn't pass me. I tried to breathe and talked to myself: *One more step, one more step. Just move one foot a bit and keep going.* I was high in the air and I was making progress, just like I had for all the steps to leave Thailand, to get divorced, to fix my eyes, to go to conferences. Everything seems impossible until you just take one step and then another. No one was forcing me to try new things. I wanted to do this.

I looked out over the water. It felt right to be back on a ship on my way to the Caribbean. I slowly went from barely breathing from terror to screaming with happiness and excitement when I realized that I was a warrior. I made it through the Sky Course.

Being onboard with Zoey, I remembered many of the things I'd loved about working on ships: watching the waves and looking out at the horizon and walking the promenade deck at sunset or late at night when the moonlight danced on the water. I felt peaceful. It was like I'd come home after a long and arduous journey to a place that was truly mine. I wasn't working, so I could stroll, swim, eat, dance, and do whatever I wanted.

For our port day in Cozumel, I picked the ship shore excursion with Sand Dollar Sports. I loved boat diving in Cozumel and had been underwater with this outfit when I used to work onboard for Princess Cruises. I was thrilled to be in the deep blue sea for two dives. I loved to drift dive, where the boat captain puts you in the water and you flow with the current. When the dive is over, the boat has followed you and you climb back onboard. I tried out my new video camera and had no issues using it or the selfie stick, but everything looked a bit blue to me. Maybe I needed to buy a red filter.

After my successful dives and camera work, I met up with Zoey and we went for a local lunch and wandered around the town a bit. I was happy to wander with her in the blazing sunshine and revel in the fact that my dives were superb. I was with a friend, and we were in Cozumel in Mexico! I did it! I'd wanted to go back to scuba, and I just made it happen.

After our sweaty stroll, we returned to the ship and Zoey had to work. I went up to the pool deck. I had noticed during my walks around the ship that there were two waterslides: Drainpipe (the orange slide) and Twister (the yellow slide). Children and adults were lined up on the stairs for their turn. I contemplated whether I could be courageous again so soon after my Sky Course success.

I had never been on a waterslide because I was terrified of everything about it. It was in water, it was fast, it was like a roller-coaster—which I also never did because they were so disorienting for me. I was afraid of drowning again. I was nervous. I went to my cabin and put on my bikini and grabbed my underwater camera and wrist mount.

I was scared, but I got in line and did my best to stay calm while I waited for my turn. I was starting to panic a bit and listened to the parents and children talking in line in front of me and behind me.

As I inched closer, I could see the top of the slide and the people disappearing into the orange tube. It seemed like we had climbed up several flights of stairs. I wished the line wasn't taking forever because I was starting to think about giving up. Maybe I wasn't this brave. I could hear the rushing water, and no one seemed to be screaming too much, but then it was my turn. I sat where the staff member told me to and felt the cool water on my legs. I was not leaving now. Children went on this. It was safe. As I left the top, I took deep breaths and then went screaming down and forgot to even turn on the video camera! But I lived, I smiled, and I was willing to go again. I waited in line and this time I turned the camera on. I still screamed the whole way, but I liked it.

Our next port was Belize, and Zoey and I went on the shore excursion called "Sharks, Rays, Barrier Reef Snorkel and Island Escape." We took the tender from the ship to shore and boarded a boat to Caye Caulker, a small island off the coast of Belize. There was a bar and a sandy beach, as well as a mangrove forest and many types of birds in a protected forest reserve. While we were snorkeling, I filmed on my new video camera. We saw many creatures of the sea, including large green moray eels, but the best part was just hanging out with Zoey and enjoying being ashore and on a vacation—not worrying every minute if something was going to tick Fred off so he would get angry or yell at my friends or throw something and generally ruin the day. Finally, I was trying new things. I had done so much already, and I was still forty-eight. Maybe my 50 Things project really was a good idea. I wondered what challenge I would accept next.

I took photos onboard at every opportunity. Fred hadn't been good about taking photos of me. He got jealous if there were more of me than him, he always wanted the photos to be the two of us together. I decided to take advantage of the ship's Dream Studios package for a formal photo session. The photographer and I went to the aft of the ship on Deck 10 by the Tides Pool and I stood along the railing while the photographer snapped photos as the sun set. We went back to Deck 7 and took photos in Liquid Nightclub and Limelight lounge. I could be the star of my own life.

This ship had a 4D movie theater. For my vision therapy, Dr. Brodney had encouraged me to watch as many 3D movies as I could. I took it as a homework assignment from our sessions. But 4D added another dimension. It occurred to me that vision therapy changed so many parts of my life. There were times I didn't notice all the small steps adding up, but my heart was healing. And now I knew could trust the information from my eyes as well.

I couldn't believe how fast the cruise went. The days were full and it seemed like I'd just gotten on the boat, but somehow our final port together was there. There would be two days at sea but still, I was already a bit sad about having to leave.

7.   Twitter chats

8.   water slide

9.   "American Ninja Warrior" course over the ocean

10.   Formal photo shoot

11.   4D movie theater

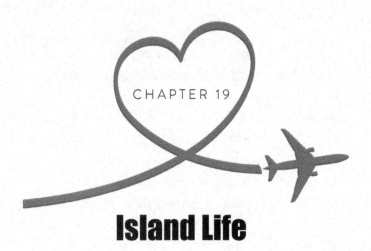

Island Life

For my forty-ninth birthday, as part of my 50 Things project, I decided to combine a series of press trips to create an epic adventure. To celebrate turning forty-nine, I planned out a month in the Caribbean, starting in Aruba, followed by Bonaire, Mexico, and Cuba. There was a time when I worried that I would never be able to do anything without Fred. Now I was alone-ish, and I loved it. I was finally feeling brave...ish.

There were nearly a dozen of us on a trip put together by the Aruba tourism board at the Divi Village Golf and Beach Resort. I self-consciously feared that I was by far the oldest, but after talking with the others, I realized it wasn't true and, undaunted, I participated in everything. We all swam together in the infinity pool, had drinks at the swim-up bar, and played on the waterslide. I was thrilled not to be afraid of the waterslide anymore.

The next morning, I woke up early to film sunrise, which was absolutely stunning. After the breakfast buffet, we all embarked on a guided art tour of San Nicolas, the second largest city after the capital.

I had read online that our resort had beach tennis. While I wasn't sure how it would differ from regular tennis, and since I had been taking lessons back in Los Angeles and wanted to keep trying new things, I wanted to play. I mentioned this to the group, and it turned out that one of the guys on my trip was a former NCAA tennis player. Back at the hotel, we went over to the sand court and I quickly realized that beach tennis is on an entirely different level of challenging. The paddle is like a giant ping pong paddle, and you need to hit the ball without it bouncing. Still, I was game. Someone else offered to film for us, and I set up my own camera to film as well.

We started playing, and while I was feeling the heat come up from the sand and not able to move quickly in the uneven ground to even try to make a shot, our NCAA player was hitting every ball with ease. I didn't give up and tried my best, but after a while, one of the other journalists came over and joined me on my side and we played doubles or two on one against the ringer. We were forced to take a break only briefly when an iguana crossed the middle of our court. I laughed a lot and probably played horribly, but I didn't give up.

The next day, we went off-roading to the Natural Pool, known as "*Conchi*" in Papiamento, a Spanish Creole language with a mix of Portuguese and Dutch, which is spoken on all three of the ABC islands. Conchi is a small, naturally occurring pool on the rugged, rocky, volcanic coastline of Aruba. It was more nerve-racking than I anticipated, but again, I was glad we went.

At the end of my time in Aruba, I flew back to Miami, where I boarded a plane for the next leg of my birthday trip: Bonaire. Scuba diving in Bonaire had been a dream since my cruise ship days. While Bonaire itself is only 113.5 square miles, there are eighty-six easily accessible shore dive sites and 100 percent of the waters and over 20 percent of the island are a protected marine sanctuary and national park. This would be my first time visiting and I'd waited for decades.

For this press trip, it was only me and one other diver—and it turned out to be her first press trip ever! Isabella was a skilled videographer and had several cameras with her. She was filling in for the owner of a blog that focused only on scuba diving. She was a dive master and going back to Honduras in a couple months to take her Scuba IDC (instructor development class) to become a scuba instructor.

For our first two days, we dove with VIP Diving, which provided a high-end scuba service called a dive butler. Our butler Jonathan put together our gear for us and carried it over the rocks to us for shore diving. He was charming and knowledgeable, and it felt luxurious to have help, and not only with our gear, but also with the absolute best spots. We parked near the long cement Salt Pier and saw an actual pyramid made of salt. When there are no cruise ships or cargo vessels alongside, the pier is home to some of the island's best diving, where you can see chain moray eels, whose scale design resembles a chain (hence the name), which are unique to those waters.

After only a few steps into the clear aquamarine sea, we descended next to the pier. Almost immediately, we encountered my very favorite thing to see when diving: a school of Caribbean reef squid, also called a shoal or a squad. Typically, dives stay around or above sixty feet, but since Isabella and I were rated for deep diving and the visibility was vast and the water was warm, we were able to descend to ninety feet. We saw two baby green turtles, Caribbean reef octopus, tarpon, scorpion fish, flamingo tongue nudibranch, and many others.

At another site called Tolo, with an easy shore entry, we were underwater for seventy-two minutes—much longer than the average dive (thirty to forty-five depending on air consumption)—

and saw vibrant corals and many different types of colorful fish. After we ascended, I couldn't wait to return to the water. All these years I had wondered if this place could possibly live up to the hype. It did.

For my last two days, I changed resorts to stay at the Bellafonte Bonaire, where the Dutch royal family stay in the penthouse whenever they visit. By the end of my visit, I was in love with the island and planned to return again for more *dushi* days. *Dushi* means "happy" or "sweet" in Papiamento.

For the next part of my birthday adventure (and list), I flew to Mexico to attend SharkSchool in Playa del Carmen on the Riviera Maya, where experienced divers can dive with bull sharks, one of the three most dangerous shark species (along with the tiger shark and the great white shark).

SharkSchool was five days long and was a combination of diving and classes. Our dive plan was to sit on the sandy bottom and stay together as a group. We would observe from there. The sharks would come quite close to the divers, and it was important to remain calm.

Each morning began at 8:00 a.m. in the dive shop, where we met to prepare our gear for a two-tank boat dive. We had our first lecture the day before and now, as we were getting ready, I got a tiny bit freaked out. I felt overwhelmed. I was supposed to try new things, not lose a finger or part of my leg.

On the first day, there was quite a bit of current. The boat was rocking, but I had been on dives with rough seas and a strong current before. I decided to trust my training. As I put on my wetsuit, set up my gear, and checked on my dive computer, I just kept thinking about shark behavior. I would look around into the deep blue, I would keep my eyes on Pascal and our dive master, Tavo. I would stay with the group. When it was time to get in the water, we were all ready and one on each side did a back roll entry into the water. Our group of twelve met at the back of the boat and started our descent. I checked in with myself, cleared my ears, and looked at my gauges and computer. *I am a good diver*, I told myself. *I can do this*. I felt comfortable in the water. I loved diving with Nitrox, which is also called enriched air or oxygen-enriched air, and is when your tank has a nitrogen/oxygen gas mixture with more than the 21 percent oxygen found in normal air. *I am well trained. I am with professionals.*

I listened to my breathing as we descended sixty feet. Our group set up in the sand without too much distance between us. Pascal didn't want the sharks to swim between us, but around our group. I watched for the behaviors Pascal had explained in our lecture. This was a different kind of diving, as we were descending and staying mostly in one place. We were waiting for the sharks to approach, and they did. It was mesmerizing to watch them. Several came by and swam around us and left. We moved to another spot and then it was time to slowly ascend to our safety stop and return to the boat. After our surface interval, we did it again. The second day was much the same. We dove in the morning and had a lecture in the afternoon. Pascal did the lectures twice each day, once in English and once in German.

On the third day, I changed wetsuits. I'd been cold, so I decided to wear a thicker one, which meant I needed more weights. The thicker neoprene would make me more buoyant, and I had to compensate. Later, while underwater in an even stronger current, I realized I should have taken *more* weight. I was not staying in one spot like I was supposed to in the sand. We were meant to sit on our knees with our fins behind us, but I was moving around. Tavo signaled me to stay put but it just wasn't possible. He gave me one of his weights. I felt terrible to be causing problems and didn't realize I was getting overheated. Suddenly, two bull sharks headed directly for either side of me. I turned to my left and realized in my bumping around I had gotten farther away from the person I was supposed to be right next to. There was too much space. I felt very far away from everyone else. Eventually, the sharks left, and I took deep breaths, trying to control my breathing better.

Normally I wasn't an air hog, but the stress of that dive had gotten to me and I never even looked at my gauges. That had never happened to me before. When we left the bottom for our ascent, I noticed that Tavo stayed very close to me until he signaled that I should go up to the boat. It was only then as I neared the surface that I realized how close to 500 PSI I was in my tank. While arriving back on the boat with that amount of air is completely acceptable, I was unprepared for how the adrenaline rush from my shark encounter and being overheated made me less attentive to my air situation. Tavo had kept a close watch on me and I thankfully wasn't in danger of running out of air. I knew that was not my best underwater moment. It reinforced how you never know what might happen next.

Back onboard, I talked about what had happened with Tavo. I still felt shaken, and I offered to skip the next dive. He assured me, "I knew something was wrong and I was watching you. Get back in for the next dive." This time, I wore my wetsuit with the zipper open so I wouldn't get too hot, took more weights, watched my distance better, staying close to my neighbor in the group, and was able to enjoy the experience. The sharks did come very near, but I was prepared and focused on checking out their behavior. Overall, it felt incredible to be in the water with the "world's most dangerous sharks."

For my actual forty-ninth birthday, I spent the day at Xplor, a jungle adventure park in Playa del Carmen with ziplines, amphibious vehicles, cave swimming, and rafting on underground rivers. I went with Sergio, my media liaison, and we spent the day doing lots of potentially-too-scary things that I ended up absolutely loving. The cave swimming and underground rafting in particular were two activities I might have easily skipped before I worked with Dr. Brodney on my eyes. I was capable and adding to my list!

At lunch time, a giant surprise awaited me in the Xplor cafeteria, where the staff sang to me and brought out a birthday cake with a huge sparkler. I was thrilled.

I spent the next day at the brand new Xenses, another adventure theme park by the same group who built Xplor, which features sensory-themed experiences and optical illusions—and gleefully warns visitors that "Nothing is what it seems!" This park would be the ultimate test for my eyes.

To my delight, I was completely capable of participating in everything throughout the park. From the carnival mirrors to the flying superman zipline, to the upside-down town and the tubes of floating mud, the day was messy, wet, and fantastic. I loved every minute of it. It was turning out to be the best birthday ever. I felt grateful for all the therapy sessions, the crying phone calls with close friends, and my own hard-won willingness to believe that things could be different. If I hadn't left Fred, I would never have had this amazing adventure.

The celebrations continued, and even my bed was decorated. The staff had wrapped towels into a tower of circles to create a cake and covered my bed in streamers, party hats and rose petals that spelled out "Happy Birthday!" I actually contemplated sleeping on the hammock to preserve it but decided to take photos and video instead. That night, I watched the stars from my balcony and thought about my wishes for the year ahead and future challenges for my project. It had started out very simply: I would try some new things. I'd known I might not get to fifty challenges, and that was okay. But the list had grown organically, and people kept making suggestions. The level of the challenges had already increased exponentially. I thought about what the next challenges might be but I also knew I wanted to wish for more dates and perhaps even a partner again. I'd been building a new life right along with my list, and on my balcony looking at the sea, watching the waves, feeling the warm coastal breeze, I was realizing that I loved it.

From Mexico, I flew to Cuba for a weeklong liveaboard diving excursion in the Jardines de la Reina Archipelago, or Gardens of the Queen. This dive spot was known for its pristine untouched reefs. Amazingly, Cuba would be the ninety-fourth country I'd visited in my life.

At this time in Cuba, travelers could stay in a *casa particulares*, which is a government-approved bed and breakfast. Right away I noticed the cars did look like a movie scene from the 1950s. A horse and carriage marched along in between vehicles. The streets were full of colorful signs in Spanish, which I could read and understand, and I could feel the ocean breeze in the air. It reminded me of most island towns I'd passed through, where many of the buildings looked a bit rundown and there always seemed to be a mangy dog or two. The street around my Airbnb seemed like war zone, with heavily pitted roads and people cooking outdoors in the street on open flames. I wondered if I'd made the right choice to come here alone or at all, but I reminded myself I'd always wanted to be here and now I was. I took a deep breath and got out of the taxi on Amistad near Neptune.

The next day, as I walked toward Habana Vieja, or Old Havana, I saw that much of the city was under construction, including Capitolio Nacional (National Capitol). On nearly every street, a restaurant opened out to the street with live music. I walked into the church at Plaza del Cristo, Museo de la Farmacia Habanera (Museum of the Pharmacy), Plaza Vieja (the historic square). It reminded me of Old San Juan and the French Quarter of New

Orleans with the archways of the buildings on the ground floor and more arches in the residences on the second floor. I saw the Plaza de San Francisco de Asís with its famous cathedral, all of the public art statues, and more music. During my visit, the streets seemed filled with songs and possibility.

I felt fortunate to be able to wander on my own without a tour guide and continued to practice my Spanish. I took photos and videos at the wide open and inviting Plaza de la Catedral, again with a large central courtyard and many archways. I walked down cobblestone streets behind groups of schoolchildren in their uniforms on my way to Museo de la Revolución.

That night, I walked on the wide, tree-lined Paseo del Prado near sunset, and on each block, a different style of music and dance was happening. There were children riding bicycles and I danced salsa in the street. I went to hear live music at El Floridita, a dance club and bar which opened in 1817, famous for its daiquiris and for being the spot where Ernest Hemingway liked to hang out to drink them. I was approached on the sidewalk by a large man who started to insist on buying me a drink. I told him politely in Spanish that I was leaving, and he let me pass. I needed to trust my instincts and focus on my safety first. I decided next time, I would come to Cuba with a group of friends so I could stay out later and be a bit more adventurous.

I was supposed to be at the hotel Parque Central, roughly three blocks away, at 4:30 a.m. the next morning to meet my bus to the dive boat. Before heading up to bed, I mentioned this to the woman running my Airbnb and asked her whether she thought it would be safe for me to walk there at that hour. She said yes, but her boyfriend who was with her, disagreed. He offered to walk me there himself, and I felt much better knowing he would accompany me.

I hadn't given much thought to my situation on the dive boat itself until I arrived at the hotel the next morning. I had met the

Avalon Cuban Diving Center team at the Scuba Show; we had talked about a possible trip and booked the dates and flights. Now that I was waiting in the hotel lobby, however, it was clear that many people were going on this excursion. It seemed like way too many for one dive boat. As we boarded the large bus, I heard Russian, Chinese, and Spanish being spoken, and it occurred to me I might not have anyone to speak to for seven days. There were almost no women among the fifty plus people and I hadn't heard one word of English. After seven hours on the bus with two comfort stops, the sun was up and we had arrived at a pier in the port of Jucaro, east of Havana on the southern side of the island.

I stepped off the bus and looked around to see three dive boats docked alongside. Standing among all these men, I felt nervous about what the group dynamic would be like.

Jardines de la Reina is a protected marine area with 150 islands; the number of divers per year is limited to under a thousand. We were heading to the southern part and expected to see Caribbean reef sharks, silky sharks, sting rays, nurse sharks, and healthy coral reefs.

There were twelve divers on my boat: ten men from Mexico, one Israeli paratrooper, and me. For my birthday I'd wished for more men, but I hadn't expected to meet them all at once! The boat set off. I was filming and listening to Spanish being spoken all around me. The ten men from Mexico traveled together every year and I was sure they were a bit wary of how one lone woman might impact their journey.

After a family-style lunch, we continued motoring into the marine park and out toward the dive sites. There would be no diving the first day. We drank sunset mojitos on the open deck together and I learned more about the men. All were married but one. The unmarried one sat next to me after dinner on the open deck with his hand traveling along my leg until it was under my shorts. His name was Mateo, and I was enjoying his flirtatious behavior. However, when his hand started to drift up my leg with his friends around us, I wondered what would happen next. He was handsome but was barely speaking to me. They were all speaking Spanish around me but so rapidly I missed most of it. It got later and darker and slowly the rest of them all went below deck to go to bed. When we were alone, I had to make a choice: Was I going to have sex on the hard outside deck with a strange man from Mexico whom I hadn't even kissed yet, on a boat that we would be together on for the next seven days, while the crew was watching? I said goodnight and headed to my room alone.

At 6:45 a.m., I filmed the beginning of sunrise. At 7:00 a.m., we had breakfast, and at 8:00 a.m., we went on our first dive of the day. After a briefing about the Jardines, we got in our two dive boats. The reefs were pristine, and the diving was incredible. During the week we saw all types of sharks, as well as damsel fish, puffer fish, parrot fish, crabs, and many corals, including brain coral, fan color, tubes, and pillar coral. We saw giant moray eels, lobsters, rays, barracuda, turtles, tarpon, spotted drum, angel fish, dog fish, blue tang, and gorgeous colors everywhere we looked! On our very first dive, the divemaster speared a lionfish and fed it to a black tip reef shark that swam by us.

Diving with all these men every day turned out to be enjoyable. They were all experienced divers, I was happy to be in the water with them, and they called me the *sirena del mar*—"the mermaid"— since I was the only female of the group. As the week went on, they taught me bad words in Spanish, and the only other women on board, the two female waitresses and room steward, told me, "Nice girls do not talk like that!" We were always together as our meals were family-style, and after diving, there were always snacks, mojitos, the hot tub, and other group activities. Sometimes I helped translate to English for Alon, who spoke Hebrew and Arabic but not much Spanish. I understood most of the diving briefings in Spanish but only some of the dinner conversation, which had many inside jokes.

I spoke more Spanish every day and started dreaming in Spanish. It wasn't until I got back home and was getting ready to write about my trip that I realized I had written all of my notes in Spanish.

The boat crew took care of us in every way. I didn't touch a fork except to eat, and I didn't touch my tank except to put my regulator in my mouth. There was no cleaning up, changing over, or work of any kind. On this liveaboard, we ate, dived, slept, and repeated. We had hot towels after each dive and were treated like royalty. This birthday bonanza of dives even led to me being quoted as a dive expert for *Departures* magazine, one of the premier travel glossies! Finally, the consequences of my actions were in the good column!

My ten male Mexican dive buddies taught me, "There are two rules of life. Rule #1: There are no rules. Rule #2: Do what makes you happy." The joy of these men together was such a stark contrast to when I traveled with Fred and everything made him unhappy. Without him, it was my rules and I was doing what made me happy.

12. Off-roading in Aruba

13. Beach tennis

14. Bonaire

15. Eat lionfish

16. SharkSchool in Mexico

17. Cave swimming and rafting underground

18. Cuba

19. Dive liveaboard (lots of men)

20. Quoted as "expert" in *Departures* magazine

Pot Party

Growing up, I was always doodling. I used to draw a cartoon character with curly hair and a shirt like a football jersey with the number fifty-one on it, and I loved to draw flowers and other squiggles in the margins of my notes at school. I took photography at camp and printmaking in high school, and at Penn I'd taken a sculpture class. But it wasn't until I dropped out of medical school and found the ceramics class by the carousel in the Golden Gate Park that I truly fell in love with art. I worked my entire schedule around it.

Between all my trips, I was still taking ceramics classes at Santa Monica College. From the very first class, I was in heaven. I loved working with clay and I loved being back in school. I already knew how to throw a pot, and sitting at the wheel felt like home.

Since it was an actual college class, there were assignments, but I just wanted to make art, so I did the assigned work as quickly as possible to be free to work on what I wanted. It might have been the first time I picked what I wanted to do over an actual school requirement. One part of class that I loved was that we were allowed—in fact, "required"—to mix glazes. There were recipes to follow, and we each signed up to make one of the standard colors for class. All the chemicals or ingredients were in the room, you just had to locate them in the haphazard cupboards. Many of the people in the class seemed challenged by this, but for me it was like being back in Chem lab. Several people asked me to help them, which I was happy to do. It all felt familiar, and I was good at something again.

After I finished the SMC class, I started a membership at The Clayhouse in Santa Monica. As the months went on, I got to know the women and the very few men at this new studio better. Raven told me she was a witch and offered to read my star chart. I agreed, and she talked to me about my plans for the future, dating, and my family. She seemed to know or notice things about me and encouraged me to focus on having fun.

One day, when I was telling her about my 50 Things Before 50 project, Raven suggested I make fifty pots and then have a "pot party." I immediately thought this was an absolutely ridiculous idea. First of all, I'd never smoked pot, so I would not have a pot party. She tried explaining, "That's why it's funny, Lisa. Everyone who knows you knows you've never done any drugs. It's a play on words! Remember to have more fun." I agreed to consider it, but it still felt presumptuous to throw my own solo art show. I mean, who does that? Turns out, that is what artists do. If you want people to see your art, she told me, you need to show it. As I pondered what it meant to be a working artist, I was also stumped by the other part: make fifty pots. I couldn't do that. It would be impossible.

"Just consider it," Raven suggested. "You don't have to decide right now."

Over the course of my 50 Things project, I'd been asked many times, "But isn't that what this whole project is about? Getting out of your comfort zone? Trying something new?" after I insisted I couldn't possibly do whatever it was they were suggesting. Afterward, however, I generally started thinking about how it might possibly work.

I decided to start keeping track of the number of pieces that I made. I really didn't know how many I could make in a month. If it was a goal to make more, and I came to the studio more often, I might be able to do it. I was traveling quite a bit now, so I wasn't sure how much time I had. Then I realized that I didn't necessarily have to make all new pots to hit the number; I could use some that I already have. Still, I wondered if I could make fifty new ones.

Raven also urged me to try some new glaze combinations. Usually, I made all my pieces with the blue and green glazes, and I told her I liked the ones I use. She said, "These are not for you. They are for your show. Other people might like other things." She also suggested I try to throw my first five-pound bowl. I didn't think this was doable or that I could possibly be ready, as I had never thrown more than three pounds of clay, but I was starting to see a pattern in my resistance. I'd already done so many new things, but every single time, I didn't believe I could do it until I just did it. What was the harm in at least making the attempt?

That first attempt at throwing five pounds didn't work well, but I kept trying. Over the next few months, I showed up as often as I could. Some weeks, I was in the studio four days and kept throwing my two-pound balls of clay and making more bowls and vases. I didn't like making mugs because of the handles. Plates are also not my go-to. I kept a list in my phone of how many pieces I'd thrown and how many were at my house.

Then I started to talk to people about having a show. I felt excited. I knew I had some pieces from before I started counting and might actually make fifty new pots to put in my show. I used new glaze combinations and tried out different ones that other people liked. I asked for lots of suggestions and just kept going. *I can do it.*

Eventually, I tried another larger bowl. One day I threw a decent three-pound bowl and another day made a mess with four pounds of clay, but I kept trying. Finally, I made something with 3.5 pounds and felt proud of my efforts. I chose to focus on making the pots for my show and not making a mess with larger pieces.

One day, my friend Alice and I both made five-pound bowls. She reminded me when the piece got too wet and suggested when to slow my wheel. I did each step on my wheel while she did them on hers. In the end, I had a really amazing five-pound bowl. I could do it. I just needed a bit more coaching and help.

As I was planning my Pot Party, I thought back to the conversation I'd had in Aruba by the waterslide, where one of the women from the PR team told me that I needed social media for my art. I put my reservations aside and created pages for both Instagram and Facebook called Simply Ceramics, a pseudo-brand extension of the Simply Science camp I'd run before my first year-long Asia trip with Fred.

As the time for my Pot Party approached, I started to invite friends and family. I didn't really think anyone would come, so I just kept inviting everyone I knew. By the end, I had invited close to three hundred people. Not all of them lived locally, but many of my friends had earlier versions of my art, which they loved and used, and I figured they would want to know about my show. The invitation was a very basic e-invite:

Lisa's Pot Party (Art Show!)
Hosted by: Lisa Niver
Saturday, November 12, 2016
2:00 p.m. to 6:00 p.m.

My parents had agreed it could be at their house, in order to make space for the tables to display my art, I needed to move the furniture around. Arranging spaces has never been my forte, and I was certainly not someone known for their interior design sense or ability to configure furniture and decor just so. I set up my art in color families. Five bowls with bright purple glaze. Four bowls and a vase half in yellow and half in orange. All the green glazes together. I had bought flowers and put them in some of my vases too. It looked really great. I was proud. There was so much art to put on the tables. Fifty pieces really was a lot to organize. Fortunately, I'd set up the art in advance.

On the day of the party, I cut vegetables, made chocolate fudge, set out wine, water, and sodas, and wondered whether anyone would show up. Amazingly, not only did people arrive, but some even brought friends. For the next few hours, I talked to my friends and their friends about my art and the glazes, and it was delightful. I took photos with people and smiled and laughed and enjoyed how much everyone loved my work.

I had thought through many parts of the show and taken photos of all the pieces in advance, but I hadn't thought much about people buying my art. Apparently, part of having a show is actually selling your work. One of my friends wanted to purchase a small bowl with a bright blue glaze and asked if I had change, but I had no cash. I had no box for cash. Someone else wanted to Venmo me but I'd never even heard of Venmo. All around, people were wanting to buy my art, take photos with me, and request or commission a different color.

I signed my pieces, accepted money, and basically sold out of all my art. For the first time, I felt *I am an artist*. Now people were asking, "When is the next show?" I couldn't believe that they wanted more, but I said I would let them know. Best of all, I'd been in such constant motion selling, signing, promising to make things, greeting people with hello or "thanks for coming" that the worries I'd had about having to talk about my divorce or dating turned out to be unfounded. At the end of the day, I posted photos on my brand new Simply Ceramics Facebook and Instagram accounts from my Pot Party, my first successful solo show.

A few months later, my parents went skiing in Park City, and when they returned to LA, my mother said, "You know, your art is as good or better as everything in the gallery on Main Street. Why don't you call them and sell your art there?" I thought to myself, *Like it's that easy.*

The next day, I sent an email to the gallery with links to my Simply Ceramics social media pages. Two weeks later, I sent a second email and called to speak with someone. The person in the gallery was friendly and gave me a different email to use. This time, someone emailed me back and told me to call the owner of the gallery who was the main ceramic artist. I spoke to him on the phone the next day and he offered, "The next time you're in town, bring me some of your art to look at." They normally carried only local artists, but since I'd been coming to Park City for decades, he agreed to consider me. I was floored. Maybe it *was* that easy.

One month later, my parents were headed back to Park City for skiing, and I was going with them. I took two bags full of my art, and my parents also brought some of my art for me in their bags. I didn't pack it as well as I thought, and several pieces were broken when we arrived. I tried not to be too upset; I could make more and still had plenty to bring to the gallery owner's studio.

I took an Uber to the address he'd given me, but when I knocked on the door, no one answered. I took deep breaths. I had come all the way here with all of these pieces. I tried to remember the instructions. I walked around and found another door on the other side, which was his studio. At first, it didn't seem like anyone was there either. I called his phone. Nothing. I was stumped. We'd had a meeting time, this was the address, it looked like an art studio. I waited a bit longer, and then he appeared.

I took all my art out of the bags, and he looked everything over. He suggested I stop signing my pieces on the bottom with a year. "If your piece is on a shelf in the store with a date from several years ago, people will think, 'Why hasn't anyone bought this?' and not pick it." He also talked to me about choosing a few styles and making them consistently. He said it's hard to be in a store or gallery if you don't have the same thing to sell. He showed me all around his studio and demonstrated how he made press molds from his own pieces so he could make dish sets.

We discussed pricing and he told me which pieces of mine he liked. In the end, he took more than half of what I'd brought, and I was thrilled. I couldn't believe I was going to be in his gallery on Main Street. This was something I had never imagined could happen.

On the first day my art was on the shelves in Park City, two of my college friends flew in to ski with me and we had a photo shoot in the gallery with my pieces in the background. While we were there, a gentleman bought one of my pieces. The woman at the counter said to him, "Would you like to meet the artist? She's here in the gallery!" We took photos together and I was smiling so much my face started to hurt.

As my travel schedule increased, it became harder to keep up with making the pots and bowls and shipping them to Utah, eventually I didn't have any more pieces in the gallery. But the experience really changed my outlook. People liked my art and would buy my art and it wasn't just a little hobby. It was a passion of mine, and if one day I wanted it to be my focus, I already know how to grow it as a business. *I have many things that I love, and I get to choose how to spend my time.* Sometimes Fred's voice would return to my head and say, "No one wants to work with you," but that voice was nearly gone. I had options and choices. Good ones. *I am a teacher, I am an artist, I am a traveler, I am a writer.*

21. Attempt and make 5-lb. bowl for Pot Party
22. My own art exhibition

I Am a Hack

I had booked my tickets to the Travel Classics conference in Arizona as one of my first fearless acts, and now it was finally here. For the last twenty years, Travel Classics had been known as the elite print travel magazine conference, and you had to know someone to be invited to apply. The top editors from specialty travel publications attend to meet with the qualified writers. I was so nervous. Of all the conferences I'd been to, this one felt the most out of my league. You needed three recent print clips to even apply. I'd been writing for my blog and USA 10Best and while I still had my column at the *Jewish Journal*, I hadn't sold any print travel magazine stories.

I'd written to Maren Rudolph, who runs the conference, to ask for permission to apply with the clips I had. I stated clearly that I wasn't sure I qualified but that I was very interested and if she gave me a chance, I would work my hardest. I also asked if she knew of a travel conference more focused on video. She agreed that I should come try it out. Attendees had to pay for flights and hotels as well as the conference fees. It was a big outlay of cash, and I hoped it would be worth it.

At the opening cocktail gathering, I learned that many of the journalists had been coming to this conference together for years and were all sharing rooms at the pricey resort. They seemed to have history together, as well as with the editors. I'd never been a wallflower after all my years onboard ships, but at this conference, I felt acutely aware of not belonging. I promised myself I could make it through one hour of socializing and maybe even make a friend.

Rather than try to hide my new kid status, I decided to be upfront about my inexperience and use it to break the ice. I kept asking people the same thing. "Hi, this is my first time at Travel Classics. Do you have any suggestions for me?" Everyone was welcoming and mostly they told me the same thing: "Follow up with the editors after the conference." Several of them went out of their way to introduce me to people.

The conference was a combination of panels and one-on-one networking sessions, and we'd all been given the opportunity to select who we wanted to meet with during the networking. I'd chosen *AFAR* Magazine, *American Way* from American Airlines and AARP, among others. I had many meetings I was excited about, but I was so nervous I felt unmoored. I knew I should be prepared to pitch but also just get to know the editors. I was making it harder on myself by seeing myself as too inexperienced to be there.

Wine was flowing at the first night's dinner, but I wasn't drinking. And in the morning, breakfast was not well attended. The few who made it looked like they'd had a long night, and several were starting to lose their voices already. I'd spent an hour in my room the night before, preparing for my networking sessions. One of the other questions I'd asked at the cocktail party was about the meetings. Most of the journalists had said to use the ten minutes to get to know the editors and not pitch stories, but several had said, "You are talking directly to an editor at a travel magazine. Bring your best pitches and see if they like them or if they can help direct you." I wanted to be prepared, so I had pages of notes.

After breakfast were panels where the editors essentially interviewed each other in different groups. One session was about luxury travel and one was about custom publishing. I took notes and also kept a separate page of questions to look up. One question was: "What is 'J-School?'" They kept talking about "J-School." In my room, I'd started crying. I felt stupid. How did they all know what everything meant? When I finally got online and realized it meant journalism school, I laughed at myself. I hadn't realized that most of these people were formally trained. I felt like even more of a hack.

Lunch that day was at picnic tables, and I felt like I was back in high school standing alone with my tray and no safe place to land. I joined a group, and the two people seated nearest me were having a conversation about how one of them now had a baby and the other was writing a book—two major, box-checking life accomplishments I feared I couldn't ever hope to achieve. Turning to my other side, I struck up a conversation with the former general manager of the Four Seasons Hotel in French Polynesia. This was better. I can talk travel all day long. We talked about where I'd stayed in Moorea and the Bora Bora lagoon, and about cruising and hospitality, but I still felt uneasy about not being able to connect with the other journalists and editors. After lunch, I went back to my room for a timeout and pep talk.

That afternoon, as I went from one editor meeting to the next and chatted with some of the other conference attendees, I began to realize that while I might not have a journalism degree, I had a lot of what teachers call "subject matter competence" compared to most other aspiring travel writers. I had spent years traveling around the world while living on cruise ships, and a total of almost three years backpacking through Asia. One editor was impressed

I had traveled to nearly all of the countries in both Asia and the South Pacific. I was only just beginning to appreciate how much I had done.

I also realized I had diving and skiing as two legitimate areas of expertise, as well as my interest in ceramics and art. An editor from *Virtuoso Life* magazine mentioned she was looking for someone to visit Taliesin, the Frank Lloyd Wright house in southwest Wisconsin, and I thought to myself, *I could write about that. Maybe there is hope for me.* So far, I'd been focusing on what other people had to offer, as opposed to seeing how my own passions might inform my stories. These other writers weren't necessarily better than me; they'd just been doing this longer.

Toward the end of the day, I met with the editor of *Delta Sky* magazine, which is like the holy grail for travel journalists. Every writer at the conference was trying to land a print feature in an in-flight magazine, and there had even been a panel featuring editors from *Delta Sky*, United Airlines' *Hemispheres*, and American Airlines' *American Way*. I told the *Delta* editor about my recent diving trip in Bonaire and explained that I was interested in doing an article about the coral restoration being funded by Fabien Cousteau, grandson of the legendary oceanographer Jacques Cousteau. She said, "Can you get an interview with Fabien? I really want him for the section 'What's in My Bag?' If you can get him, I will assign you that story." I was inwardly jumping up and down. A print feature in *Delta Sky* would be a major coup! But I kept my cool and simply said I would investigate and get back to her.

At dinner that night, I sat with Nick, the editor from *Hemispheres* magazine for United Airlines. I asked about the editor pet peeves from his panel, I just couldn't believe that after all the effort writers made to get a story, they commonly turned things in late or not at all. I told Nick I'd really wanted to meet with him, but we hadn't been matched for an appointment. He kindly said, "Lisa, I've met you; I know you're not crazy. Just email me your pitches."

I was terrified to meet with the editor of *Luxury* magazine because everybody said she was very particular and didn't want anything. I took lots of notes while she talked on the panel earlier in the day. When we met, I spoke with her about the villa where I'd stayed in Bonaire called Studio Piet Boon. I followed up with her immediately after the conference since I knew *Luxury* still paid three dollars a word—a rarity in the magazine world—and she immediately sent me a contract. I was going to be in *Luxury*!

I finished the conference feeling like a small but bona fide success. I had overcome my insecurities and made new contacts, learned a lot about the print magazine world, and had several legit leads for pieces. Back in Los Angeles, I reached out to Fabien Cousteau's team, told them I had a potential print story, and as soon as I set up the interview, the editor at *Delta Sky* sent me a contract. I had just sold my very first ever print story to one of the best magazines in the business.

After the conference, I also sent a pitch to an editor I'd met from *Sierra Club*, and in a P.S., I wrote, "Next week I won't be online much because I will be in Park City, Utah, skiing with the blind,"—something I'd wanted to learn more about ever since seeing the skiers wearing orange pinnies that said "Blind Skier" when I was a kid. She emailed back, "I want that story!" I thought to myself, *That wasn't even a pitch.* But I corresponded with her and before I knew what was happening, she had sent me a contract to write the story.

I wrote to Maren to thank her for allowing me to come to the conference and apologized for only selling three stories. I told her that nearly every editor had suggested they might be interested in something we'd discussed, and I followed up with each one several times. She wrote me back immediately. "Lisa, most writers sell no stories, some sell a single story, and nearly no one sells THREE!

You did a great job. Thank you so much for your fun videos from the conference. I love having those great memories. Looking forward to seeing you at our international conference in Ireland."

23. Sell first three paid print articles to "Delta Sky, Luxury," and "Sierra Club" magazine

Ready on the Set

My trip to Park City to go skiing with someone visually impaired—now officially an assignment for *Sierra Club* magazine—had come about thanks to a chance encounter on a recent weekend ski trip with my family. On the chair lift, I'd met a woman who worked for the National Ability Center, and as we chatted on our way up the mountain, she talked to me about their work with skiers with different challenges. I asked, "Are you talking about the people who wear the orange pinnies that say 'Blind Skier?'"

"Yes, I am."

I'd grown up seeing these skiers on the slopes and wondered if I could learn more or even volunteer. I followed up after the trip and asked how I could participate. She invited me to ski with one of the NAC lessons the next time I was in town.

In my pre-trip research, I learned that the National Ability Center has been changing lives for over thirty years by helping families who have children or adults of different abilities find a way to participate all together in the outdoors. The NAC programs are inclusive and multi-faceted, and they run year-round teaching skiing, snowboarding, horseback riding, and river-rafting. According to the CDC, one in five American adults live with some kind of disability, and many others have differences in their physical, cognitive, or developmental abilities. The NAC has programs for people of all ages and ability levels, and they are brilliant at devising ways for their participants to be on the river or on the mountain.

Patricia, the lead ski instructor and trainer who had been working with the NAC for many years, told me I would be skiing with her and her student Jennifer, who was blind. When Jennifer and her husband moved to Utah from New York City, Jennifer had wanted to learn an outdoor sport and discovered the lessons through the NAC. She and Patricia had been skiing together weekly, and Patricia was training Jennifer's husband to be her guide.

Everyone got their gear on, and we skied the short downhill to the beginner chair, First Time. Patricia gave many verbal directions to Jennifer.

The first step was to build trust. Patricia had done this by walking, then skiing, backwards and maintaining glove-to-glove contact to give Jennifer confidence as she experienced sliding on snow. When Jennifer was ready, they both held a long pole horizontally, to continue building confidence while listening to verbal commands. As Jennifer's faith in her ability grew, the pole was put away and she skied independently listening to promptings to turn or stop. As we started down one of the beginner green runs, I could see that Jennifer was already a proficient skier. Graceful and confident, she followed all of Patricia's cues with relative ease, and we slowly made our way down the slope. I was impressed by her progress and Patricia's teaching style.

I enjoyed my time on the slopes with the NAC and wanted to write about more of their programs. Patricia recommended I ski with another one of their top instructors, Chris, who would be teaching one of the veterans in a wheelchair to use a monoski later in the week.

I'd been able to shoot some video while skiing with Jennifer and Patricia, but trying to ski and film at the same time had been a challenge. Before my next outing with the NAC, I reached out to the Park City Mountain public relations team and they offered to partner with me and handle the filming and editing for this next experience if I would host the video and promote it.

On the day I was scheduled to ski with a Wounded Warrior, I arrived at the mountain early to prepare for my special team filming experience. It turned out I was going to have not one cameraman but two!

We walked out onto the snow and my two cameramen first filmed me talking about our day, so we would have a beginning and end to our video. Next, we headed over to meet Matt, a wounded warrior who had lost both legs above the knee in 2012 from injuries sustained during his military service in Afghanistan. He was learning to use a monoski, which looked like a wheelchair attached to a single ski. It didn't seem like it could work, but he would use two outriggers which looked like ski poles that each had a small ski on the bottom. Those three points of contact on the snow would keep the skier balanced. Matt had agreed I could follow his lesson with the camera crew and film him. He'd been skiing for several years but had been using a different system called a bi-ski, and this was his first time with the monoski.

After one or two trips down a beginner green run, we headed over to a blue intermediate slope. Matt and the instructor went over some bumps and Matt fell. I was worried about him, but he laughed and said, "What's the worst thing that can happen? I'm already in a wheelchair." He looked at me and grinned, "It's not like I can break my legs or have never been in a hospital."

After a few more runs, it was time for the terrain park where there were jumps, jibs, and half-pipes. I'd never been in one in my entire life. Chris encouraged me, "Lisa, you can do it. Just stay to the side, watch your speed, and roll over the bumps instead of jumping." I took a deep breath and followed them in.

At the end of Matt's ski day, he spoke with me about his military service, his injuries, and how NAC had helped him return to being active outdoors. It was an honor to ski with him, talk to him, and share his story. After we wrapped filming, the two cameramen told me they would work on the edits, music, and the chyrons, or the people's names or information that appears in the lower part of a video image.

I took an Uber to the Olympic Park to bobsled for the first time, and on the ride over, I told my driver about my day skiing with a Wounded Warrior. He said he was former military as well, so I thanked him for his service and we talked about how I skied with Jennifer, who was blind. The closer we got to the bobsled, however, the more I started to panic. What was I doing? This was not just some roller coaster or waterslide. This felt serious.

I told my driver, "Maybe this is a bad idea. Maybe I shouldn't go."

He responded, "You spent the day with someone who had the guts to ski while blind and you won't sit behind a professional driver for less than one minute? It's a tourist attraction. It has to be safe. You will be fine!"

With the tough-love encouragement of my Uber driver ringing in my ears, I walked into the building and went to register. The bobsled team was expecting me. I signed my waiver and was shuttled to the finish dock of the bobsled track for orientation and group assignments. Each bobsled would have a driver and three passengers.

As we stood huddled on the dock, the team told us this would be a "highly physical and extreme experience." In motion, our bobsled experience would generate up to two to three times the force of gravity. They strongly discouraged anyone with chronic neck problems, back or kidney problems, heart problems, recent surgery, and/or high blood pressure from riding. Furthermore, anyone questioning their health status or experiencing hesitation should not ride the bobsled. Please note, they continued, that there is a possibility of injury whether the above listed conditions and symptoms apply to you or not.

Of course, by this time I was regretting my decision. But I wasn't leaving. I had my winter clothing and gloves on and I wanted to be brave. I wanted to challenge myself. That was the whole point of my 50 Things Before 50 project. *I can do it. I just have to sit there and try not to get hurt or die from terror.*

Jessie, the track coordinator, had given me the seat in the number two position behind the driver, and she promised it was the "Cadillac," or best position, where I would be least buffeted and rocked by the many g's of force I was about to experience. *How did I get myself into this?* I nearly backed out multiple times. There would be 3 g of force, she told me. It used to be more, but people were getting hurt and throwing up. You could still get hurt from being thrown about during the quick ride, so they explained how to brace ourselves in the sled.

My professional bobsled driver said, "Lisa, I've been on this track more than three thousand times. I am an expert driver." I stood staring at him from a distance. "Lisa, I will bring you back. I promise. You have to sit down now." I finally took my seat. Turning around, he said, "You can scream as loud as you want. It won't bother me at all."

I wondered if I would scream loudly on the bobsled, but once we shot out of the gate, the g-force on the run was so great I could barely breathe, let alone scream. For 47.38 seconds, we zoomed around the track at speeds up to sixty-five miles per hour. The track curves went flying by as I was tossed from side to side in the metal tube and the force pressed me deeper into the seat. It was a short, intense ride—incredible, memorable—and when it was over, although I was glad I did it, I doubted I would choose to do it again. I had conquered my fear. As I regained my equilibrium and readjusted to moving at a speed that was *not* sixty-five miles an hour, I had one final thought: *Olympians rock!*

I discovered that *The Jet Set* TV show hosts were searching for travel stories and exciting interviews, so I pitched myself and my 50 Things project. I told them I'd been scuba diving with bull sharks and skied with the blind. They invited me for an on-camera television interview—my first ever—if I was ever in the DC area. Willow, whom I knew from my San Francisco days, was now in DC and I asked if I could visit and stay with her. She said, "Of course!" I wrote back to get more details and work out a date.

I flew myself out for *The Jet Set* TV interview, figuring this could be a steppingstone, another opportunity to be on camera. Every time I was on camera, I improved. Television is one of those things you learn by doing. I arrived fifteen minutes before my call time at the studio, and as I stood on the set, waiting for the production team to call me over, I felt the thrill of being on set. Nikki Noya, who would be interviewing me, said, "I've read all about your adventures and I cannot wait to talk to you."

When the next person entered the studio, I suddenly heard, "Oh my God! Is that Ms. Niver-like-Diver the science teacher?!" It was the mom of one of my former students from Curtis School. She was there to do a luxury fashion interview for a product. She gushed about how I was the best science teacher either of her girls had ever had. After all her raving about me, I just hoped my segment went well.

Our interview focused on "Transformation Travel" and Nikki asked me how I got started on my project of doing fifty new things before fifty. I explained, "This project has inspired me to be more excited about turning forty-nine and now about turning fifty...to tell the truth about my age." She asked me about diving with bull sharks in Mexico, and I told her, "I was really nervous, and I even cried before I got in the water the first time. But I did it, I loved it, and I'm still trying new things."

Nikki asked if I'd been anywhere new. I told her about scuba diving in Cuba and Bonaire, and we talked about how I want to go back for lionfish hunting and a moonlight dive with the ostracods.

"I loved being in Bonaire so much I thought about moving there!" Then she asked me about other great underwater experiences, and I told her, "When I was in Palau, we dove at a site called the Blue Corner. They developed a reef hook to keep you in one place and protect the reef, so you are hooked on a line in the strong current and you fly like a kite in the water as sharks and turtles and fish swim by you! It was one of my best dives ever."

Then she asked me to talk about one of my greatest experiences.

"It was an honor to interview Fabien Cousteau, the son of Jean-Michel and grandson of Jacques Cousteau." She asked me how to begin as a travel writer, and I said, "If you want to write about travel, you have to just start. I am now running my twelfth international travel writing competition and I've published more than two thousand writers on my website. People often tell me it's hard to take the first step, but I recommend they dip their foot in the writing pool by entering one of our contests. They don't have to build a website or social media platform. They can write one story and share it and see how that goes."

After my segment, Nikki and Bobby told me I'd done a great job. I said, "If you ever need any travel or adventure segments, I would be happy to come back and share more stories."

Bobby looked at me and said, "Be careful what you wish for. It might come true!"

Back in Los Angeles, the Vail Group invited me to Kirkwood Mountain south of Lake Tahoe for the annual two-day Expedition Kirkwood Women's Ski Clinic. The Kirkwood Clinic was for women who wanted to make rapid progress, learn new skills, and ski better, harder, and faster. All the instructors had been working with ski teams and women's clinics at Kirkwood for over twenty years. Everyone tackled new terrain or gained confidence in conditions they would not attempt on their own. Over the course of the day, Amy, one of the leaders, suggested I'd sold my skills a bit short and could easily have gone in a higher-level group. She said, "Women often pick a group lower than their ability whereas men will overrate themselves. Tomorrow, I want you to try a higher group." I timidly agreed.

Before our second day of the clinic, there was an overnight storm, which meant we were snowed in and the coaches for our clinic were snowed out. The roads were completely shut for most of the day. Looking out my window, I saw the resort crew digging out the chairlifts, which were buried in snow. It was my first time ever being snowed in anywhere, and some of the women in my group were saying that getting snowed in at Kirkwood was on many top skiers' bucket list for the pristine conditions and limited number of people. If the roads are closed, no one else can get in and you can get out there and make first tracks. When Chair 5 was dug out and in operation, I skied with Teodora and Alusha from the group above me and they led several of us through the white-out conditions. I greatly appreciated their guidance and we had an epic day together. They led our group through the fresh powder and trees, areas I'd always avoided previously, being fearful of the narrow passages.

From Kirkwood, I went on to ski at Heavenly and Northstar resorts, two additional Vail resorts in the Lake Tahoe area. At Heavenly, which spans two states, I skied in both California and Nevada in the same day. At Northstar, I met my friend Ellame, the Vail resorts PR person, for the very ritzy Platinum tōst with cheese board, champagne, and s'mores with homemade vanilla bean marshmallows, served outdoors at the top of the mountain. We enjoyed the sunshine, comfortable beanbag chairs, and relaxation—all slightly surreal given that we were in full ski attire.

Ellame said, "I'm glad you came to our three mountains in the winter. I want you to come back this summer for Pumps and Pedals, which is our women's mountain biking weekend." I looked at her and practically screamed, "I am not coming for that." She continued telling me how great it was, but I told her I'd had a bike accident as a kid and there was no way I was doing it.

"Even if you get me a private lesson with a teacher who doesn't mind crying, I will say no."

But then she said the magic words. "I've never gone either. I'm scared also. What if we do it together?"

24. Ski in the Terrain Park

25. Olympic bobsled

26. First television interview with *The Jet Set* TV

27. Snowed in!

CHAPTER 23

Keep Your Eye on the Ball

With the *Jet Set* TV segments and all my videos on various platforms, my profile was steadily growing. I'd been working with Amazon Direct video and Roku and, altogether, I had one million views across all the platforms, including YouTube. I met with a PR friend who suggested I separate my views out.

"No one can verify your views on Amazon Direct or Roku. You're saying you are over a million views but then they look on your YouTube channel and it's less than that—it looks like you're lying." I would never lie about my views, and I don't want there to be confusion, so I followed her advice.

I was being viewed as an "expert," and media invitations and travel opportunities kept coming. At this point, I needed to be more particular in figuring out which events to say yes to. There were almost too many invitations. But I happily kept going to parties and wore lots of sparkles.

When the next request appeared, I was certain I was being punked or on that long-running television show *Candid Camera*. The email was from United Airlines, and it looked real, but it was an invitation to attend the Oscars and sit in row A on the red carpet! I called and spoke with Robert from United Airlines, who confirmed it was, in fact, a real invitation. United Airlines was flying in the statues, and they chose five travel or "Oscar" bloggers to join them at the red-carpet event. And to think that only two years ago I had been worried I would never go anywhere or do anything again without Fred.

Our Oscar Fan Experience Day started at 10:30 a.m. because we all had to go through security and be in our seats hours before the stars arrived. There was live entertainment and Maybelline makeovers, manicures, photo stations, swag bags, and box lunches to eat.

By 2:00 p.m., we had to sit and remain in our bleacher seats on the red-carpet sidelines ready to record the stars' long walk down (partially in the rain). The most surprising moment was when Lady Gaga was walking down the carpet and turned around to glare at whoever had dared to accidentally step on her train—before realizing it was Oprah.

At 6:00 p.m., we went to El Capitan across the street to enjoy the 87th Academy Awards on the big screen. A dinner buffet, popcorn, and drinks were given to us as we sat in our comfy seats to see who had won each Oscar. While it had been exciting to see the stars, the real thrill of the experience for me was being included as an Oscar Blogger for United Airlines.

My next surprising invitation was from the Japanese National Tourism Organization (JNTO). It was not surprising they were inviting me somewhere, as I had gone to their annual events before and really enjoyed them. One year it had been at the Japanese Museum in downtown LA, and another year it was at the Dolby Theater with a tour of the Japan House gallery. This year, however, the JNTO was inviting me to watch the LA Kings play hockey from a private suite. I was not at all sure what hockey had to do with Japanese tourism, but I'd never seen a hockey game, either live or on television, so I was an instant H-E-double-hockey-sticks YES and secured a ticket for me and a plus one.

I brought along my Brazilian friend, Renata, who had no clue about hockey either. We knew we needed warm layers but as we were going to be in a suite, we dressed up too. Before the game started, we went down on the floor and watched the players warm up with our noses pressed against the glass. I had grown up watching figure skating on TV and was amazed at how these massive, mountain-sized men could move gracefully and nimbly on skinny little blades. I loved the music and the crowd and could not wait for the game. Back in the suite, we sat next to another writer, Dawn, who had been watching hockey with her family for her entire life. She gave us a quick tutorial that helped immensely, and I was ready.

Hockey is fast, but for the first time ever, not only could I see the puck, but I could also follow the game. Suddenly I understood why everyone watched the sport. I loved the non-stop action and the men jumping over the wall of the rink to get on and off the ice. They kept playing even when their sticks broke! At the end of the third period, the score was tied two-all so there was overtime, and then an eleven-round shoot-out! Of all the sports I'd seen, hockey was now my favorite. It was fast-paced and entertaining.

The next month, I went to my very first NCAA Women's Basketball game and saw my own college team, University of Pennsylvania, play at Pauley Pavilion at UCLA. I was having such a good time going to sporting events, that I joined my parents, my sister, and her husband to watch the football game on parents' weekend at USC where my nephew was a college student.

While all of these new sports were great, scuba diving was still my true love. I'd stayed in touch with a woman named Susan, whom I met at the Long Beach Scuba Show and really wanted me to write about diving World War II wrecks for the seventy-fifth anniversary of the Battle of Guadalcanal. I'd never been to the Solomon Islands so I pitched the idea to *The Jet Set* TV show, who agreed to a segment that I could film while I was there.

I flew to Fiji and had a few moments of panic in the airport when I arrived, because I came face to face in the baggage area with the spot where Fred and I had our first huge fight about how I'd eaten butter on my bread during the flight. I hadn't been back to Fiji since that trip, and now I wondered if this was a good idea. I'd never experienced place-memory like this before and was viscerally upset. I took deep breaths and told myself that was in the past, and I deserved all the good things in my present, including being on my way for a private two-week press trip.

The Solomon Islands is an archipelago of nine hundred islands with six hundred thousand people, ninety languages, and nine provinces located between Papua New Guinea and Vanuatu.

I traveled to three islands: Gizo, Munda, and Guadalcanal. And on each, I went scuba diving, visited war memorials, and learned about the local culture. My first dive site on Gizo was Toa Maru, a Japanese transport ship and one of the most frequented World War II shipwrecks to explore in the South Pacific. Inside the ship, you can still see a telephone and medical supplies in the hold.

On our way back to the resort afterward, we stopped by Kennedy Island, a teeny tiny, uninhabited island very close to Gizo where John F. Kennedy had swum to safety after his patrol boat was struck and sunk by a Japanese destroyer in 1943.

On Munda Island, our wreck diving continued and included two planes, the Airacobra wreck and a Douglas SBD Dauntless dive bomber, both American. During our surface interval, we went to Lubaria Island, which had been a forward base for JFK during World War II. At Skull Island, a short ride from Munda, we saw evidence of headhunting, with skulls that ranged in age from three hundred to one thousand years old.

In Honiara, the capital of Guadalcanal Island, I had been specially invited to witness the creation of shell money, an antique form of currency similar to coin money that is still used in some island provinces today, primarily for ceremonial use but also for bridal and land payments. Only the people of Langa Langa Lagoon can make shell money. The women allowed me to attempt the steps with them and I could see what fine artisans they were.

I went back underwater for two days in Honiara with Tulagi Dive for a deep dive to 130 feet—the outer limits of recreational diving—and a deeper dive into history with the Japanese I-1 submarine.

At Lumatapopoho Cultural Village, a traditional settlement in Honiara where the islanders still lived as they did hundreds of years ago, I felt like I was stepping back in time. Chief Primo and his wife, Paula, shared their traditions with me. When I arrived, there was a greeting welcome betel nut ceremony and then Primo showed me their kitchen and their homemade bowls from hard wood. When he showed me how they made fabric from tree bark by taking the fibrous strips and beating them with a mallet, I wanted to try it. I asked him, "Can I have a turn?"

Primo laughed and looked at me strangely and kept going.

I asked, "Are women allowed to help make the cloth?" because I wondered if only men were allowed to do it.

He said, "No, women can do it. Do you really want to try?"

I said, "Yes! Definitely."

He laughed again, and said, "Lisa, no visitor has ever asked for a turn." He handed me the mallet, and as I started beating the strips of bark, I felt like it would take a tremendously long time to turn this piece of wood into something wearable. He said, "You are doing a good job."

He also showed me how they could make an entire house from local materials in the jungle. He was able to sew the roof together using sharp pieces from a palm tree; it looked like staples when he was done. Alternating bamboo and vine created a colorful weaving pattern on the walls. Inside the building they had spears so I asked if I could hold one and then we took photos together. Chief Primo told me, "Lisa, you are a warrior now!"

My local guide, Anna, helped me film my segment for *The Jet Set* TV, and when I returned to LA, I was also able to pitch and sell my story and videos about the seventy-fifth anniversary of the Battle of Guadalcanal to *Smithsonian Magazine*. I was elated to have gotten a TV segment and an online feature out of the same trip. Then my dad said, "Would it help your story if you could interview someone from the Battle of Guadalcanal?" Apparently, he had a new patient named Roy Roush who had been a soldier in the battle. I arranged for the interview and was able to sell the story to the *Saturday Evening Post*.

28. Oscars Red Carpet
29. Hockey game
30. First visit to the Solomon Islands
31. Make fabric/shell money, the Chief said I am a warrior

Return and Learn

Unfairly, in my mind, so many of my travel adventures were linked to Fred. At first, after the divorce, it was easier to go places that were completely new, a blank slate, uncomplicated by Fred memories. But eventually new opportunities in familiar places started to pop up, and I had to decide whether or not to take them.

Joanne Vero from Travel Media Showcase, the conference in Texas where I'd first decided to embark on my fifty things project, invited me to the Sugar Sand Festival in Clearwater Beach, Florida. It reminded me of the Konark sand art festival in India, which Fred and I attended together on our second long trip to Asia—and where I'd first decided to start my travel writing competitions. The Sugar Sand Festival seemed like it might trigger a host of uncomfortable emotions, and I worried about going, but I also didn't want to say no to Joanne, who had been supportive and helpful and believed in me all along.

I flew to Florida, hoping for the best and telling myself it would be a great trip. The sand festival, which was in a tented area on the beach, had taken eleven artists eleven days to build, and one thousand tons of sand. Fantasy was the theme, and the creations were out of this world! One of the artists was still in the process of building, so I asked if I could help. I jumped right in to shovel sand with him even though I was wearing a dress. For our sunset dining experience later on, we ate at a table made of sand with a sand bench shaped like a dragon's tail with scales and a dragon head. The sun went down in a flash of spectacular color, and we had fresh fish tacos, marvelous music, and all got up to dance.

It was a good day, but throughout it all, I had flashes of the festival in Konark. I felt anxious and off my game. At one point, when I moved files on my hard drive to make room for new photos before we all went to the Clearwater Marine Aquarium, I accidentally deleted important files. Fortunately, my new friend Jason, another travel writer, offered, "Lisa, if you are too stressed to go on this tour, go back to the hotel and figure out your computer. I will take photos for you." He was kind and supportive, and reassuring about the fact that people make mistakes. He had made mistakes too. Fred had always used every opportunity to say that something was my fault, as if he'd never made a mistake in his life. I realized that even if I had made an error, it didn't need to ruin the day or cause DEFCON 1. Being upset would not bring the files back. I pulled myself together, resolved to deal with the files later, and went on the tour.

The Clearwater Marine Aquarium focuses on the rescue, rehab, and release of marine animals, and they care for dolphins, turtles, manatees, and river otters who've been injured, before returning them to the water. We took a boat tour that taught us about the animals, the estuary, and the mangroves, and the children on our tour were able to touch creatures, observe a net pull, and identify fish. I filmed Jason during a stop on a sand bar, because he wanted to get into a video, and didn't wallow in my tech mistakes.

That night, there was going to be an outdoor concert by Kenny G at Coachman Park. I had been a fan of Kenny G since college, but I also wanted to hear Jake Shimabukuro who was the opening act. Jake is an incredible ukulele player who plays his four-stringed instrument with astonishing skill, and his music sounds like the most breathtaking acoustic guitar. When you hear him play, it seems impossible that a ukulele could produce such sounds. The hitch was that I only knew about Jake because of Fred, who had played the ukulele as well as the guitar and introduced me to Jake's music. I had many memories of Fred playing the ukulele when we traveled together and, in truth, it had given us many cool experiences. Often, people approached us when he was playing, so his music had helped us meet locals and fellow travelers. And he was an excellent musician. We would be somewhere, and he'd pick up an out-of-tune guitar with a missing string and play it and it would still sound good. It hurt to think about these things, but I didn't want the associations with my ex to ruin this chance to see a live performance.

I believed I could go to the concert and let go of my past relationship associations with the ukulele, and I was right. It turned out to be an amazing outdoor experience; the park was beautiful, and the music was exceptional. Jake played first, and then Kenny G gave an amazing show. He played multiple instruments and told stories about how life takes practice and a sense of humor: If you keep practicing, you will get there. You need to have passion, but you also have to work. I loved these life lessons and felt like he was speaking directly to me. They say that music heals the soul, and that night I realized I could keep the music in my life if I wanted to. Ukulele and guitar didn't belong to Fred, and I did not have to lose them even though I'd let him go.

Asia in particular was loaded with Fred associations, but I knew I couldn't avoid the continent forever. In April, I received an invitation for a VIP press trip to Shanghai because China Eastern Airlines wanted to show off their new business class. I was hesitant, but it seemed nuts to pass up going to China even if was just for a weekend.

My group met Wednesday night at 10:00 p.m. at the LAX International Terminal, and we enjoyed the spacious seats, free Wi-Fi, and snacks in the Korean Air lounge while we chatted and waited for our turn to get on the Boeing 777. We boarded shortly after midnight early Thursday morning. Since we were crossing the dateline, we would arrive Friday morning in Shanghai and return on Sunday to Los Angeles.

We boarded early for photos and champagne, and after take-off, we had a choice of Chinese or Western entrees for dinner, and after a long sleep, another choice of Chinese or Western entrees for our breakfast. When we got off the plane and compared notes, each of us had been told they were out of something, and when Jeana had tried to order the Chinese breakfast, she was told, "No, you cannot have that. Your friends ate too much. No food for you." She was able to get something else but we still decided this crew might not be quite ready for primetime or Western business travelers.

After we disembarked at Pudong International Airport, the other writers and I followed our guide to China Eastern's Diplomat line, a speedy VIP entry into the country. We sailed through immigration with our leader and were rapidly on our way to downtown Shanghai. Outside the terminal, we walked to the depot for the futuristic maglev train, which looks like something from *The Jetsons* and runs up to a speed of 268 mph (430 km/h) with an average speed of 155 mph (249.5 km/h). The ride between the airport and downtown Shanghai takes exactly 7 minutes and 20 seconds, and as we whizzed over the tracks, I videoed the speed of the train on the monitor in our car. After our short ride, we stepped out and were met by our transportation to the Waldorf Astoria Shanghai in the historic waterfront district of the Bund.

I'd been worried about returning to Asia; however, once we arrived, I felt comfortable, like I was right where I belonged. At the hotel, the front desk needed our passports. Often on group trips, because everything is paid for, you aren't even required to check in at a hotel or put down a credit card. The front desk will just hand you a key. But this was China, and I knew that they would not be so casual. In China, they often do more than just check the passport, they usually photocopy it or sometimes even keep it. I handed mine over instinctively, but others in the group were not doing the same. The supervisor came to speak with me, and I redirected her to our group leader who was from the New York PR firm who had arranged the trip. Still the passports were slow to materialize. Finally, I walked up to one fellow who was standing around and told him to give me his passport. He hadn't understood this was required. I urged him to get it out, and then took it to the front desk.

Everyone was impressed I seemed to know not only what to do with the passports at the desk but also Mandarin—because I kept telling everyone who worked at the hotel, "*Xie xie*" (syeh-syeh) which means "thank you." Before I knew it, I had been pegged as the de facto tour leader, with everyone asking me for advice about what to do and where we should go.

That morning, a top tour guide from Abercrombie & Kent led us through former British banks and other buildings in the Bund district while we learned about the history of the area. Later, in the Tianzifang art district, we all photographed the flower-covered walkways, the mango drinks with dry ice, and enjoyed the people watching. Yu Garden, the verdant oasis in the center of Shanghai that had been built in the Ming Dynasty more than four hundred years ago, reminded me of the Summer Palace in Beijing, where I had traveled with Fred. I simply acknowledged this similarity and let it go. As was my habit with new people, I had not mentioned Fred or being divorced. I truthfully told people I'd visited Shanghai when I worked on ships and picked up my Chinese language skills when I was traveling in China for six weeks with a friend. I was feeling proud—I'd thought I would never get back to Asia, and here I was doing it all on my own, leading the group, and feeling strong and assured.

The following day, we explored the French Concession and walked through a large park where a giant group was dancing to what sounded like Chinese swing music played by a man with a stereo and several speakers. Harold, from my group, and I both found partners and started to dance while my another friend Jeana filmed for me. The park was thrumming with passersby and people doing tai chi, women pushing strollers and little kids watching the dancing. I put my ballroom and salsa skills to work as my partner twirled me around. Afterwards, Harold, who only danced briefly, said to me, "I didn't know you could dance."

I thought to myself, *We just met and there are many things you don't know about me.* But I told him, "I love dancing!" It felt good to affirm this part of myself. I danced for quite a while and with several partners. At night, we went outside to enjoy the stunning skyline and buildings of Pudong with its colorful electric light display. Our hotel location was perfect for walking to the best sights.

Most of my group had napped during the day but I did not. I wanted to film and went for a walk while the others slept. I was too busy enjoying being back in China, but once we sat down for dinner upstairs in our hotel, for an intimate authentic Chinese meal featuring Cantonese, Shanghainese, and Huaiyang cooking in a dark, quiet room, the jet lag hit me, and my eyes kept trying to close. I left before dessert and took the short ride on an historic elevator back to my suite.

On our final night, we went to the Long Bar in the hotel which has been open since 1911 and has live music, classic cocktails, eight types of oysters, and a wonderful atmosphere. While we were there, a man came up to me suddenly and said, "Lisa? Lisa Kozel?" Now, *that* was confusing. I mean, "Lisa Kozel" had been my married name, but I was divorced and in China. It turned out to be Fred's best friend's younger brother, who did business regularly in Asia. "I read your travel newsletters and I love your YouTube videos. It's great to see you. Tom will be glad to know you were here traveling."

My friendly and curious group invited him to join us for a drink, but mercifully his boss showed up and they were shown to their table. I simply told my group, "He is my ex's friend's brother." And changed the topic. No one seemed to have noticed he'd called me a different name, or perhaps they could tell from my pale face that I didn't want to talk about it anymore.

In *The Lion King*, the shaman Rafiki says, "The past can hurt. You can either run from it or learn from it." I hoped I was learning. There were moments that gave me cause for concern about how my past was informing my present, but I'd been able to adjust and reinvent my experience of Asia, just as I was reinventing myself.

32. VIP on China Eastern Airlines

33. Maglev train in Shanghai

Squealing Brakes

The next time I was in New York, I stopped by the office of the Ogilvy PR team to thank them for sending me to Dublin. While I was there, I met the account director for the United Nations project called Champions for Humanity. They were looking for influencers to help them raise awareness for the first ever World Humanitarian Summit, which was designed to address how humanitarian assistance is given to refugees around the globe. They invited twenty of us to the UN to learn more about their project, and they wanted us to use our social media feeds to raise awareness and promote humanitarian action. That was how, a few weeks later, I walked into the lobby of the New York Headquarters of the United Nations, and heard an overhead announcement say, "The Security Council is now in session."

After my years of participating in Model United Nations in high school, I could not believe that I was at the actual UN. I felt a bit like Dorothy in the *Wizard of Oz*, as though I had simply clicked my heels and magically wound up somewhere that I had always wanted to be.

I entered a conference room that had been set aside for our group and was delighted to see my name in lights on a little screen in front of my microphone, just like the ones used by the diplomats. I felt honored to be included and recognized as an expert. When you go to medical school, you get a diploma and a license, and you do a residency, and there are all sorts of steps to be credentialed as an expert along the way. But for a travel blogger, how do you know you're doing well? How do people differentiate you from someone else? At the United Nations, countries come together to solve the problems of the world. It seemed like confirmation that I had reached a new level of visibility and expertise.

While I was in New York, Riley from Ogilvy PR recommended me for a Satellite Media Tour (SMT). An SMT is a series of television and radio interviews that take place during one day from a single studio and coincides with morning news programs. My first project was for Hilton Garden Inn, I knew the Hilton team from past projects, and it turned out to be both lucrative and a great learning experience. After hair and makeup, the tech asked me which ear I wanted to wear my earpiece in, I said, "Right." I'd never worn one before but figured, what difference does it make? *Play along like you know the part!*

When I was offered the chance to do a second SMT, I again flew to NYC. Unfortunately, while I was in the air, the project got canceled, and when I landed, I found out there was no filming. A writer friend from Penn invited me instead to a travel event at Hakkasan, which offers world-class Chinese dining. I misheard what she'd said and thought it was an event about Macau. However, when I arrived and got confused, I said, "I'm here for the event about Morocco."

The woman at reception looking at me quizzically and said, "Do you mean the event for *Monaco*?"

That didn't sound right to me, but I said yes. My brain was searching itself for information on where in the world Monaco was, and what it was famous for.

Monaco is located on the southern coast of France and known for its Formula 1 car racing. But the new thing they were promoting was the Formula E, car racing for electric vehicles.

Shortly after the New York event, I attended a similar event in Los Angeles and assisted them in inviting local writers. At their invitation, I attended the New York International Auto Show and had a virtual reality auto racing experience. Gildo Pallanca Pastor, CEO for the Venturi Automobile race team asked me, "Will you be joining us in Monaco for the Formula E race?" And just like that, I was on my way to the e-Grand Prix.

Monaco was my ninety-seventh country. With an area of only 0.81 square miles, it is half the size of New York City's Central Park and the world's second smallest and most densely populated country. Situated on the French Riviera, it is only eight miles from Italy and seven minutes by helicopter to Nice. It has the highest per capita GDP in the world and is known as a playground for the rich and famous, thriving as a tax haven for both individuals and foreign companies, and is renowned for the casinos in the district of Monte Carlo.

I was staying at the Fairmont Monte Carlo Hotel, a historic bastion of old-world European glamour, and my garden room had a view of the renowned Casino de Monte Carlo. There was also a famous rooftop pool called Nikki Beach, from which I could look down and see the iconic racecourse laid out below. On my first day, I did a walking tour of the city, and watched the changing of the guard at the Prince's Palace. The Formula E race the next day was my first car race of any kind. My expectations of burning rubber and loud engines were supplanted by quiet cars lapping the track with relatively little drama. The most famous part of the traditional Formula 1 race is a hairpin turn called the Fairmont Hairpin that is considered the most dangerous part of the track and runs right by the Fairmont Hotel. But at the time, the electric cars didn't have the horsepower to get up the hill to the hairpin, so they had to modify the course.

For my return helicopter transfer to Nice, I arrived early at the base and was told I could leave immediately with another group or wait until my scheduled time. The woman at the ticket counter said, "I think you should wait as you will be the only passenger and have a private flight!" As we lifted up off the helicopter pad, I thought to myself, *If that second satellite media tour had actually happened, I would never have met the team from Monaco, and never had the chance to fly over the French Riviera and view the blue Mediterranean by helicopter. Sometimes, it's better when things don't work out.*

Now that I was writing about the world of racing, more car opportunities continued to appear. I was invited to Palm Springs to drive a BMW coached by a professional race car driver. I had always been a cautious driver due to my eye issues. But now that my eyes were better, maybe I could try it. There are only two BMW Performance Driving schools in America, one in Thermal, California, where I went, and the other in South Carolina. My professional race car driver and instructor was Christopher Hill. He'd won a Formula race, participated in the league of champions, and been on a car racing reality show called *American Hot Rod*.

The first part of our experience was performance driving, where my fellow classmates and I drove a variety of cars on the track and learned about car control, cornering, and timed laps. He was coaching us by two-way radio. All the cars were set with traction control and dynamic stability control. Chris explained where to position the seat, when to brake, and how to use paddle shifting.

I pressed down on the accelerator as I approached the orange cone where we were supposed to turn. I slowed to round the corner and Chris urged me over the radio, "This is not your car and these are not your brakes. I want to hear them squeal!" The next time I got to a cone, I was less timid. We were to speed up on the straightaway and keep accelerating until the next cone. With each lap, I went faster and drove the car harder. Over the course of the day, I drove the BMW 240, M4, X3, X5M and X6M. It was liberating to focus on speed without my fear holding me back.

At one point, it started drizzling. I mean, it never rains in California. As I went into one turn, I felt the wheels give just a bit and I thought, *Am I going to crash this beautiful and expensive car right now in front of my coach and the other class participants?* My heart was racing and I thought, *This is a mistake!* But I trusted the machine and it turned out fine. When I finished that run, I got out of that car and into the next one. Christopher helped me adjust the mirrors and my video camera and I went out again. I was doing it. I was on a racetrack.

For the second part, we did a closed course timed challenge in M3s with a 440-horsepower competition package. The timeclock is sensitive to one-thousandth of a second and I showed great improvement. My first lap was thirty-nine seconds and my final lap was thirty seconds! The record was twenty-six, and I finished second on the podium. I had raced a high-speed car and done well.

For our final ride, Chris said, "Put on your seat belt and hold onto your hat," because we went drifting! Invented by the Italian race car driver Tazio Nuvolari, drifting is a driving maneuver in which the driver intentionally oversteers with a loss of traction when going around a corner. I had seen professional drivers do this in the movies but never imagined I would be in a car that drifted! I enjoyed feeling like I was on the set of *The Fast and the Furious*. I felt comfortable on the course and was proud of my improvement. When I'd dropped out of med school, I never imagined someday I might be driving a BMW race car.

34. Guest at the United Nations

35. Monaco (and my first car race!)

36. BMW race car driving

Solo(ish)

After Monaco, I returned to the Travel Classics conference in Kilkenny, Ireland. The international conference apparently drew more high-profile editors. Planning this trip felt different from my first trip to Ireland two years ago. Last time I had been with a group and was falling apart emotionally and sleeping with questionable men. Now I was focused on placing articles and moving my career forward.

As Monaco was my ninety-seventh country, I decided to add to my fifty things project to travel to my one-hundredth country. With this focus, I planned a trip to Scotland after Ireland, and then San Marino, a landlocked microstate situated within Italy near the resort town of Rimini and the Adriatic coast.

At the conference in Kilkenny, I tried hurling, an ancient stick-and-ball game that started three thousand years ago and is unique to Ireland. It's played with a wooden stick called a hurley and a ball called a sliotar that is slightly larger than a tennis ball. This is the national sport of Ireland and people are very loyal to their home hurling team. Previously, I would never have attempted a new sport with a ball, but after beach tennis in Aruba, I agreed to a lesson. This wasn't even close to a real game, which has a field twice the size of a soccer pitch and fifteen players on each side. Nevertheless, about a dozen of us went out into a grassy area and the instructors explained how to play. We each had our own hurley and I tried my best to follow the rules.

You can't pick up the sliotar with your hands, only with the stick, but you can kick the ball, catch the ball with your hand, pass it to someone else, and carry the ball, but not for more than four steps. It seemed like the grandmother of all sports because so many things were allowed. We practiced trying to scoop the ball up with our hurleys and also striking the ball when it was hand-passed to us. After several attempts, we tried to move the ball down the field. As the ball was lobbed towards me, I sometimes hit it and sometimes missed. I believed I was quite terrible, however the locals in my group told me how well I was doing.

We went to dinner at Mount Juliet Estate, a manor house in the countryside outside Kilkenny, where the greeting by the family's hounds was so enthusiastic they actually knocked me over while I was filming them. After the conference, we did a tour of the Wild Atlantic Way, the famous, rugged, coastal route that runs up the west side of country from Cork to Derry. We stayed in Ashford Castle, which dates back to medieval times and is now a luxury hotel. I walked the grounds, filming everything, and learned about the history and the ghost stories from the local team.

The Hawk Walk at Ireland's School of Falconry was the best part of the trip. The lead trainer, Tommy, taught me about the school's Harris Hawks, the most popular bird used in British falconry, called "the sport of kings." I put on giant leather gloves called gauntlets that allow the hawk to perch on your arm while protecting you from their sharp talons. The majority of falconry gloves are left-handed because in Medieval times, you would have used your right hand to hold the reins of your horse. I walked into the woods with a six-year-old hawk named Joyce on my gloves. She was calm but very alert and looked at me intently. I was mesmerized; I had a bird of prey sitting on my arm. The highly-trained birds performed perfectly. When I lifted my arm like Tommy taught me, Joyce flew away, and when he put meat back in my glove, she returned. I had never been up close to a hawk or done anything like this. Even though there was adrenaline rushing through my body, I was able to selfie film the entire thing. My one-woman band was just as competent as the hawk. I had now been filming long enough that I could have confidence that what I captured was high quality.

In the seaside town of Sligo, we went to dinner and a poetry reading at the house of a local resident named Damien Brennan. He and his wife offer "The Yeats Experience" with local Irish fare while he reads from the poetry of William Butler Yeats. Their cottage overlooks Lough Gill, the lake that is home to the Lake Isle of Innisfree, made famous in Yeats's beloved poem. One of the men in attendance was watching me film my intro for the event, and afterward, he came up to me and said, "You're going to want to do that again."

I was surprised, but I am open to critique so I asked, "Why am I going to do it again?"

"His name is spelled Yeats but pronounced *Yates*—I figured since you said it incorrectly, you would want to do it again." I was glad for the assist because I truly hadn't known anything about Yeats before this evening. I thanked him and redid my introduction.

The next day, there were two options: surfing or the VOYA Seaweed Baths. Learning to surf was something I was considering, but Ireland didn't strike me as a top spot for my first lesson, so I went with the seaweed bath. This three-hundred-year-old Irish treatment had been brought back into use by Sligo local Neil Walton, who had opened a spa called VOYA. I enjoyed my slippery seaweed bath, took photos, didn't drop my camera, and made sure it didn't look too much like I was making an X-rated film!

At Sliabh Liag (or Slieve League), the highest sea cliffs of County Donegal, I understood why people traveled from far and wide to walk the Wild Atlantic Way. Peaks of nearly two thousand feet topped with patches of Irish green plunge down into the deep blue waters below. Sliabh Liag is truly spectacular. On this second trip to Ireland, it hit me again how much my life had changed, and how much my efforts to build my career were paying off.

After Ireland, I flew to Scotland by myself, where I had never been. For this leg, it was just me—no group, no PR team. No help. I was a true solo traveler, completely on my own and loving it. I could go wherever I wanted and talk to whomever I wanted. It was all me. Me, me, me.

I arrived in Edinburgh from Dublin on Ryanair and took the tram from the airport to Haymarket, a lively, historic neighborhood west of the city center. The weather was sunny with a clear blue sky, and I strolled to my hotel in short sleeves. I thought, *Why am I worried if I can do this myself? I am a great traveler.* With my local SIM card, I was able to access maps on my phone and easily navigate the ten-minute walk from the station. I walked everywhere in the days that followed.

On my first afternoon, I walked along the Royal Mile, the main thoroughfare of the old town, which runs between Edinburgh Castle and Holyrood Palace and has been the processional route for kings and queens for the last five hundred years. I loved listening to the bagpipe players on the street corners, wandering into St. Giles' Cathedral to see the stained glass, and watching local children play with bubbles on the street. When I was hungry, I ate at a restaurant. When I was tired, I sat down. I didn't check with anyone or ask anyone for their opinion. I didn't do anything that wasn't my first-choice activity every single minute of the day.

At night, I went back to my private room in a local hostel. This was my first time staying in a hostel by myself. I had stayed in plenty of hostels when traveling with Fred; hostels are inexpensive and often have shared rooms and baths. One of my greatest fears when I left Fred—and perhaps one of the reasons I married him in spite of the red flags—was that I wasn't sure if I could travel alone. I knew about traveling on cruise ships, but not the backpacker trail in the *Lonely Planet*. Now, I was doing it by myself and even staying in a hostel rather than a fancy hotel, and I was doing just fine.

I planned to be at Edinburgh Castle, one of the oldest fortified structures in Europe, when the One o'Clock Gun was fired. Since 1861, ships had set their maritime clocks by the gun, or cannon, which is still fired every afternoon at 1:00 p.m., except on Sundays, Good Friday, and Christmas Day. I was there, ready and filming, and it was *loud*. Today, the castle is the headquarters of the Royal Regiment of Scotland. There are jewels, a prison, and a war history museum, but the views from the top of Castle Rock, the volcanic outcropping on which the castle itself sits, were seared into my memory.

The Great Hall, which was the inspiration for Great Hall at Hogwarts in the *Harry Potter* book series by J.K. Rowling, contained a hall for banquets which is still in use. I had read it is worth looking up at the five-hundred-year-old ceiling, because it's the upside-down hull of a ship. If you have the largest navy, you want to show off your ships. In the armory, there was a display of all types of swords and suits of armor, and the Scotland crown jewels, which include the oldest crown in Britain. I also saw the scepter, which was presented to James IV by Pope Alexander VI in 1494, while the crown was first worn for the coronation of James V's wife, Mary of Guise, in 1540. They were first used together for the coronation of Mary Queen of Scots in 1543 when she was nine months old. I learned about how the jewels were kept secret from

1651 to 1660 to hide them from Cromwell's Parliamentarian army. In 1707, after the Treaty of Union between England and Scotland, they were locked in a chest and sealed away, but in 1818, the novelist Sir Walter Scott found the jewels along with a silver wand. I felt like I was walking in the stories from *Outlander*!

For my third day of walking tours, I went to the Palace of the Holyrood, which is the official residence of the British Monarch in Scotland. Learning about the life of scientist Maria Sibylla Merian in The Queen's Gallery inspired me. Her expedition in 1699 to Suriname made her one of the first people ever to plan a journey rooted solely in science. She traveled with her two daughters and spent two years in South America painting and doing research which led to her major work, *Metamorphosis Insectorum Surinamensium* (de), in 1705, for which she became famous. Sir David Attenborough considers her to be among the most significant contributors to the field of entomology. I enjoyed that I could linger as long as I wanted in this exhibit and savor every detail.

While in Scotland, I found out I was a finalist for the Los Angeles Press Club's fifty-ninth annual Southern California Journalism Awards in two categories: Print Column, for my article in the *Jewish Journal* about my divorce, "A Journey to Freedom over Three Passovers," and Travel Reporting, for a story called "Mongolia: Land of Dunes and Moonrises." I had joined the Los Angeles Press Club on the advice of a friend as a way to make connections and find new outlets for my writing and videos. I couldn't wait to go to the awards ceremony and cherished that my writing was being recognized as award worthy.

After Scotland, I flew to Bologna and took the train to the beach town of Rimini, on my journey to my ninety-ninth country, San Marino, which has no airport or train station. I would take the bus to San Marino to get my passport stamped before spending the day exploring. It's the world's oldest surviving sovereign state, the third smallest state in Europe after Vatican City and Monaco, and the fifth smallest in the world by land area—only Vatican, Monaco, Nauru, and Tuvalu are smaller.

The 2017 Games of the Small States of Europe were happening and being hosted by San Marino. Summer Olympic games for Europe's smallest countries—Andorra, Cyprus, Iceland, Liechtenstein, Luxembourg, Malta, Monaco, and Montenegro, as well as San Marino—had been held every two years since 1985. Athletes competed in nine events, including swimming, gymnastics, and cycling.

When I got off the bus in San Marino, I took the blue and white tourist train up the hill. Città di San Marino, a medieval settlement on the slopes of 750-meter-high Monte Titano, was founded by a Christian stonemason named Marinus in AD 301 and added to the UNESCO World Heritage list in 2008. There are medieval stone walls around the town, and I started my walking tour by visiting the three iconic fortresses along the ridge. I visited Tower #1, also known as Rocca o Guaita, and saw athletes in their country's jackets. I spoke with the Monaco judo team and told them about my recent first visit. The Iceland cycling team gave me tips for when I make my first visit there. At the visitor's center in Piazza Garibaldi near the Basilica del Santo, I was able to get my passport stamped for five euros.

I strolled along the cobblestone roads to visit the town's other piazzas, including the Piazza Sant'Agata, Piazzale lo Stradone, and the Piazza della Libertà. As the sun went down and I boarded the bus back to Rimini, I thought about how I'd reached ninety-nine countries, forty-two things on my list of challenges, and been nominated for not one but two awards. Fred had stolen a lot of my belief in myself, but I was becoming more of a believer every day.

37. Hurling in Ireland

38. Ashford Castle for falconry

39. Scotland: Country #98

40. Stay in a hostel by myself

41. Two-time finalist for the Southern
California Journalism Awards

42. San Marino: Country #99

Get Out of Your Own Damn Way

In June, I was delighted to win second place in the Southern California Journalism Awards' print category for the *Jewish Journal* story about my divorce. I'd had mixed feelings about writing it and sharing my saga, but it resonated with people who'd read it, as well as the judges. I still struggled to accept the idea I was smart enough and good enough at what I do, but now I was gaining confidence that I was competent to compete with seasoned reporters.

My friend Ellame reached out again about mountain biking. She knew about my biking accident, my eyes, and the horrible Bagan biking trip with Fred I had written about for the *Huffington Post*. After she said we could take a lesson together, I agreed, with trepidation, to join her for a mountain biking lesson in Lake Tahoe. Meg, my instructor who outfitted me in all of the gear, took me and my bike out to a grassy glade to start working with me. While it was hot and tiring in the dry summer heat, that was not my problem. The problem was that I was missing skills. In mountain biking, you stand up while you pedal. Standing pedaling allows you to generate more force when climbing hills and going over different terrain. You can shift your center of gravity to remain balanced, and change gears, but I had never stood up on bike pedals.

Meg said I would need to learn several skills before we went up on the chairlift. But despite her careful instructions, I wasn't even getting step one.

Ellame and I had agreed in advance that "Whatever happens, we tried." It was okay not to make it all the way. Ellame and I went into the shade, had some water and PowerBars, and got ready to turn in our gear. We came, we attempted. Baby steps.

Sensing my resolution to give up, Shep, the owner and lead instructor, came over to us and said, "Let's go up the mountain."

"Nope, we can't go up. Meg said I needed three skills. I have no skills."

"Let's go!" Shep said, louder, and somehow, he convinced us to follow him. I figured I could always ride the chairlift back down the mountain. He couldn't make me get on the bike. It would not help my story if I got hurt.

Shep was encouraging, reminding me that the trails would be suited for beginners and to not worry about what was ahead—focus on the now. Up the chairlift we went. And out on the trail, Shep was my guide. He explained the skills to me again and said I didn't have to stand on the pedals if I didn't want to. Slowly, when I felt like it, I tried to follow his instructions. I focused on the basics, pedaling and braking, and if he said to change gears, I did it, rather than worrying about when to do it. He went ahead of me on the trail, and I went along behind him, becoming more comfortable on the bike. I was filled with pride that I didn't give up. Not only was I struck by how beautiful it was up there, but also how well I was doing. Ellame was biking along behind me, and Meg was in the rear.

I had been promised only green beginner runs, but Shep suggested we move on to an intermediate or blue trail. I peeked ahead and the path looked scary, with a much steeper slope, full of rocks and dirt. I hesitated, but I did trust him. Surely, he wouldn't take me somewhere to die before my fiftieth birthday. I told him, "This project isn't 'fifty things until one of them kills me.'"

He looked over at me. "Lisa, your comfort zone is like this," and he held up his two hands clasped tightly together. "I am trying to help you have a bit more space." He moved his hands slightly apart.

At the turnoff to the trail, I was fairly certain I was going to hyperventilate and pass out. Shep looked at me and asked, "Have you fallen? Have you gotten hurt? Has it been too hard?" The answer was no. I'd listened to him. I had not fallen. I was not hurt. I was smiling. I could do this. I was doing it. I realized that I was already a better biker than I'd ever been before and getting familiar with the ins and outs of riding. And, even more importantly, I realized that by just saying yes to mountain biking, I'd taken great strides in overcoming the fears that arose out of falling off my bike onto my head decades earlier.

I wiped away my tears, took a deep, raggedy breath, looked at him and said, "You're right. I'm not hurt. I can do it." And I agreed to do the blue trail. Shep went first and there was a giant rut in the path. I watched how he handled it and started onto the trail. I screamed the whole time as I went down and into the divet (a small depression or hollow), stopping in a very inconvenient spot, but I did not fall over. I kept cursing. I took more deep breaths and started again, but I'd lost the downward momentum from the hill and had to pedal hard to get out of the rut. But I did it. I made myself look out over the green grass and up at the blue sky and notice the picture-perfect white clouds. I had picked this day. I had picked these challenges. I got out of the divet and onto the steeper part of the slope, picked up speed and screamed as I sped downward, letting my bike handle the road. It felt like I was flying. I was in control, and I was going down a ski slope on a bicycle! I hoped

I could make it all the way to the base of the trail in one piece. I smiled big at Shep and continued down to the bottom.

At the end of the day, I reflected that mountain biking was by far the biggest challenge I'd accomplished on my 50 Things Before 50 list so far, and the one of which I was most proud. I could have left after the bunny hill, and it would have still counted as an accomplishment. Ellame and I celebrated by going out for ice cream together. I didn't know it at the time, but she had undergone treatment for a glioblastoma brain tumor seven years earlier and was now having a reoccurrence. But she had a *carpe diem* philosophy. When she'd said we could go mountain biking together, she shared her strength with me. She was truly an incredible warrior, and her friendship changed my life.

43. Mountain biking

Vegas, Baby, Vegas

Most of my 50 Things before 50 challenges had come about fairly organically. I was at the women's ski clinic and learned about Pumps on Pedals, or I'd missed out on the Satellite Media Tour but ended up at the event for Monaco. However, there was one bucket list trip where I decided to search for access—an African safari. I wrote to Abercrombie & Kent USA, the world's leader in luxury safari travel, to express interest in learning more and was invited to a meeting in Las Vegas during the Virtuoso Conference, a conference for travel agents. Of course, I told the marketing team, "Yes, I can take that meeting." Then, I worked on a plan to get to Vegas.

My Vegas experience brought me multiple bigger-than-life opportunities. I flew in on JetSuite X, called "everyone's private jet" because it offered a semi-private air travel experience with commercial fares. I had several lavish spa treatments, and the MGM team, who knew I was an experienced diver, invited me to scuba dive with the sharks in the Shark Reef Aquarium at Mandalay Bay. I imagined my favorite part would be seeing all the sharks up close, but it was interacting with the kids on the other side of the glass.

They gave me high fives, and the little girls jumped with joy that I was in the tank with the exotic sharks and other creatures. I smiled and danced with them.

The next day, I walked into the gym at the Mandarin Oriental, and as I walked toward the treadmill, a gentleman asked me, "Do you like Monaco?" I found this to be an odd opening line and I told him so.

He said, "Your bag says Monaco on it."

"I went to see the Formula E race."

"Do you like fast cars?"

"Yes!" I exclaimed.

"Do you want to drive a race car today?"

I assumed the correct answer was, "Yes."

Mysteriously, he said, "Meet me in an hour over there," and pointed to The Crystal Shops, the fancy mall that was a part of the Aria/Vdara complex across the street.

"I don't want to buy a car."

"You're not going to buy a car," he explained. "You are going to drive a car. Just go change into long pants."

"But I don't have any pants," I said.

"You can still drive. We'll dress you in a race suit."

It turned out that this man was Enrico Bertaggia, a former race car driver who now owned Dream Racing, a five-star driving experience that offers people the chance to drive exotic cars on a real race track. At the Las Vegas Motor Speedway, I signed all the release forms and admitted to the man behind the desk that I had no idea what kind of car to pick to drive. It turned out I was speaking to Cédric Sbirrazzuoli, another renowned race car driver, who looked at my name and then at me in my dress and said, "Don't worry, I know what car you're driving." Not only would Cédric be my instructor, but I would also be driving his award-winning car.

The Lamborghini Huracan GT was a bona fide racing vehicle and considered perhaps the fastest GT on the planet. It is a true, non-street-legal racecar, and before I took it on the track, I watched a video about the course and practiced driving the car in the simulator with a video of the track. Cédric sat next to me and explained how it would work. He was impressed with my ability to shift in the simulator.

When the practice was over, I walked to the vehicle, which was impressive, and had a photo shoot in my race suit with the Lamborghini Huracán GT and my world-famous driver Cédric Sbirrazzuoli beside me. My seatbelt and helmet were triple-checked and it was time to go.

I stalled. I stalled again. But the third time was the charm and I got the car into first gear. I'd been told in advance it would be noisy, but I didn't notice. I heard only Cédric in my headphones because I was hyper-focused. I was trying my best to pay attention and paddle shift up and down, but I still occasionally had some confusion about right and left from my eye issues, and at one point, I accidentally downshifted instead of up. Cedric assumed I couldn't hear him clearly and I let him believe this was why I'd made the error. We continued around the track and he said, "I'm going to talk to the other coach on the track." He had different channels on his headset. I only had one—him.

He told me to speed up. I was intently focused on doing whatever he said correctly because I didn't want to crash his racecar with him in it. I was now traveling at 120 mph on a closed track. I was a race car driver!

Then he said, "Okay, now we are going to pass that car."

I briefly thought, *The instructions were "Do not pass another car,"* because I am a rule follower. Then I thought, *His car. His rules.* I passed other vehicles on the race track at the Las Vegas Motor Speedway. Not bad for the girl who grew up believing she was clumsy and unathletic. That night, I was ready to celebrate my rockstar-ness at Jean Georges Steakhouse. I was treated like a celebrity and had an amazing dinner.

My next amazing food experience was a cooking lesson with the Michelin three star-rated Chef Pierre Gagnaire at Twist at the Mandarin Oriental.

I was invited into the kitchen on the twenty-third floor for my private lesson with Chef Pierre, who told me, "My goal is to put tenderness on every plate." He said the most important things were "to respect the guest and have a great team in the kitchen." I was able to mix sauces, plate the food and, of course, take photos and videos. They got me an apron and a tall white chef's hat. I truly looked the part!

After Vegas, I headed to Charlotte, North Carolina, for the next Travel Media Showcase Conference. This was the conference where back in Grapevine, Texas, I'd met Tammilee and decided to consider doing my fifty things project. Now I was back, having come so far; I had already completed challenge number forty-five!

At the opening night cocktails, I saw Leigh Lyons, who had run the conference in Grapevine. There was some discussion in our group about a grand prize being awarded for stories and content that had come out of that conference. I said to her, "If I'd known there was a contest, I definitely would have entered."

She replied, "Don't worry about it."

On the second night, we had an evening event at Southern Grace Distilleries, which crafted small batch whiskeys. Leigh was up onstage talking about the grand prize winner of this contest I had apparently forgotten to enter. She started to list the content that this person had created based on the last conference. The titles were sounding very familiar to me. As she continued to read,

I realized they were the titles of all the videos I had created and posted online.

When I went to the front of the room to accept my award, I stopped and grabbed Joanne Vero, the founder of the conference, to come with me. I said, "You deserve this award as much as me, because if it wasn't for you, I would definitely not be here."

Joanne gladly skipped to the front with me and then spoke about me to the group.

She said, "Last year, Lisa told me with tears in her big blue eyes that she wasn't sure travel writing was going to work for her. I told her to keep going and here we are with her winning the Grand Prize for content with her fantastic travel videos."

44. JetSuite X, "everyone's private jet"

45. Cook with three-star Michelin chef Pierre Gagnaire

CHAPTER 29

Safari Searching

A friend shared an opportunity to do a travel segment for KTLA Channel 5, the biggest local station in Los Angeles, with an audience for their morning news coverage larger than the national shows. I met Kimberly Cornell, an Emmy Award–winning producer, and we chatted about several possible segment ideas. Major fires had happened in Napa Valley and some of the news coverage made it appear that every single structure had been decimated. I suggested we focus on this area that needed positive coverage of the fact that over 90 percent of the wineries and area were still open. She explained to me I needed to arrange a giveaway that would include hotel, restaurant, flights, and activities for two people.

My PR friend Aaron, whom I'd worked with since 2014 when I first returned to LA from Asia, was quickly able to negotiate the hotel stay for my segment at Hilton Garden Inn Napa, California, as well as a Hertz rental car for four days. The PR team for JetSuite X was in for the roundtrip "private travel" flights for two. WhichWinery, a company that created experiences around wineries, offered two activities, including Winemaker for the Day at Raymond Estates and the Luna Elevated Experience Tasting tour at Luna Winery. I called the Napa tourism board, and they made the connection for a hot air balloon ride from Napa Valley Balloons for two. It quickly came together, as people trusted me, and all my networking and past experience was paying off.

When it came time for my studio taping, I wrote out a complete script with details about the giveaway, as well as information and possible questions to ask about Napa. I printed two copies to bring with me and sent it by email to my producer as well. I took the information I was sent about my onsite contact and instructions for where to park and when to arrive and created a "call sheet," listing the times, phone numbers, and all the instructions. I printed it and put it in my folder for the day. I brought a second dress, shoes, and different earrings. I did my own hair and makeup and planned to arrive early.

At the gate, I showed them my call sheet and received my parking and visitor's passes. I took photos with every single sign that said KTLA. Kimberly arrived dressed head-to-toe in sequins and advised me to pick the more sparkly earrings for my interview. We would be taping a "Look Live" segment—it was filmed in advance to look like I was in studio and live but had the advantage of doing several takes and editing. I'd even printed my We Said Go Travel logo and put it in a frame to have on the table next to me in case that would be in my shot. Kimberly was impressed with my thorough paperwork and that we shot my "Look Live" in one take.

She asked me, "How would you feel about going live?"

"How do *you* feel about it? If you think I am ready, I am *ready!*"

Many people I knew saw the segment, and my uncle even recorded it and played it at our family Thanksgiving dinner.

Soon thereafter, I was invited on a safari to Tanzania and Kenya to several recently renovated Sanctuary Retreats properties by the

PR team for Abercrombie & Kent, whom I'd met with during my trip to Vegas. I was close to accomplishing both fifty things *and* visiting my one-hundredth country—Tanzania would be country #100 and Kenya, #101.

It would be my first time on safari, and I packed and repacked the bag A&K had sent. We had a limited amount of luggage we could bring, and it had to be soft-sided due to the small aircraft we would be traveling on in between resorts.

At the start of my long-awaited adventure, I flew from Los Angeles to Amsterdam and then on to Kilimanjaro International Airport in Tanzania. Our group stayed one night in the town of Arusha before flying on a six-seater plane to our first safari camp: Sanctuary Swala, in the middle of Tarangire National Park. When we saw a herd of elephants from above during the short plane ride, I realized this was going to be great. Sigi from Sanctuary Retreats picked us up in a jeep from the airport and our first game drive started immediately.

The land in Tarangire was flat African plains dotted with trees and brush. Within minutes, we saw more elephants and several babies. I was thrilled to realize we were close enough to the elephants to take selfies! Observing the animals while they were walking, drinking, and moving around was mesmerizing. I loved seeing a zeal of zebras, and the different types of animals near each other. Watching the majestic giraffes walk right in front of me brought me great joy.

My two favorite things on safari were watching animals cross the road and seeing the baby animals. After our picnic lunch under the acacia trees, we saw another parade (herd) of elephants and a leopard. On our first day, we saw two of the Big Five! At 5:00 p.m., as we were headed to our camp, we saw African buffalo, making it three of the Big Five on our first day.

Sanctuary Swala was our home for the night. Our stunning luxury canvas tents had every amenity, including both an indoor and outdoor shower. We were taught how to call for someone to walk us to the dining area after dark: you take a flashlight and shine it into the trees. There are no fences at Sanctuary Swala, so there are animals all over the camp. I loved the meals with a view, the pretty pathways, the animals close by, and my very comfortable bed.

We only had one night there, so in the morning after breakfast, we flew from Arusha to the Serengeti, Tanzania. Zebra lingered on the airstrip. After our flight, we got in the next safari jeep. After only a few minutes, we saw topi, a type of antelope. They looked like they were wearing blue jeans.

I was thrilled to be able to charge the batteries for my camera in our jeep, but when I opened my camera to change the battery, my SD card full of my videos and photos literally leapt out of the vehicle and onto the ground next to us. I started to climb over the side of the car to get my card full of photos when our guide yelled, "Lisa, *stop*! You cannot get out right now." We weren't moving. We were watching a mother and baby elephant. Nearby stood a bull elephant, who our guide worried might charge at us. He asked us to be very still. He promised he would collect my card when it was safe. Matt, a professional photographer, asked me, "How did that even happen?" I had no idea. Obviously, I didn't intend to lose the card with all the photos. Fortunately, the elephants continued their walk across the road, our guide collected my card, and I promised to be much more careful in the future.

When we came close to our next safari camp, we saw our first olive baboons, banded mongoose, and gorgeous scenery with a crocodile or two. I didn't realize how many different kinds of animals we would see and how frequently we would see them.

At Sanctuary Kichakani, we stayed in what are called "tents." The outside is canvas, but on the inside it's a large luxury hotel suite full of amenities. To use the fancy bucket shower, you arrange a time for the hot water to be delivered to the regular-appearing shower on the inside of your tent. The details and the comfort in my tent were impressive, and during the night, we could hear lions roaring nearby. I wanted to stay forever.

In the afternoon, I spotted a bee-eater bird, which impressed my group and myself. My eyes were working in ways I never imagined. We saw water buffalo, wildebeest, zebra, and when we stopped at the high ground above a hippo pool, we were allowed to get out of the safari vehicle and watch the dozens and dozens of hippos at sunset.

I was learning the language and, in the morning, we all said, "*Jambo!*" which means "hello." For our all-day game drive in the Serengeti, we hoped to see big cats: lions, leopards, and cheetahs. On the way, we saw olive baboons, giraffes, zebra, warthog, wildebeest, hartebeest, dwarf mongoose, and gazelles. Our guide, Filbert, brought us to an area where, in the distance, two lionesses lurked in the tall grass. We were the first safari truck to arrive. Our patience was rewarded as the lions came closer to where we were. We could see there were also two cubs frolicking.

It was surprising when one lioness suddenly had a Thomson's gazelle in her mouth, and even more so when the two lionesses started to fight over the kill. During the rest of our day, we saw four more lions, a leopard in the top branches of an acacia tree with his kill of a Thomson's gazelle, as well as herds of zebras, elephants, and giraffes. And then Matt, the incredible photojournalist in our group, told me he loved one of my photos of the leopard in a tree with an antelope carcass. I definitely could not have done this before I worked on my sight.

I learned to say *asante sana*, which means "thank you," to Filbert for the most amazing day. *Lala salama* means "good night," *simba* means "lion" in Swahili, and *hakuna matata* ("no worries") is real too. The men of Sanctuary Kichakani broke into song while I was learning Swahili. They sang so well.

After my serenade, we left our mobile tent camp and flew from Seronera Airstrip to Tarime Airstrip, also in Tanzania. We traveled overland and crossed out of Tanzania and into Kenya.

Africa was a grittier, edgier experience, more like what Fred and I did, and nothing like Monaco or Ireland or Las Vegas—places I had been traveling most recently. It reminded me of some of the better things in my time with him. I hadn't been sure I would ever think positively about our time together after things ended unbelievably poorly. There were many ongoing issues, but there were moments of togetherness and travel that I'd learned from and was starting to remember fondly. While leaving him was the right choice, I was able to now gain perspective and recognize the good times we had.

Our next stop was Migori Airstrip, with the first of several small planes on our journey from Sanctuary Kichakani in Tanzania to Sanctuary Olonana in Maasai Mara, Kenya. For our game drive with Duncan, we went through Oloololo Gate and explored. We saw elephants, zebras, a lion and a lioness together, a water buck, a single large male lion, spotted hyenas, a solo lioness, grey crowned cranes, warthogs, a brightly colored kingfisher, and many elephants. We were hoping to find a rhino to complete our sighting of the Big Five.

In the Mara, we saw cattle because the Maasai warriors have herds of them. Before we visited his village, I asked Chief Richard for permission to bring my hula hoop.

He said, "What is a hula hoop?"

I showed him a video of the team at Sanctuary Kichakani trying out my hula hoop by the campfire.

He laughed and said, "Yes!"

When we arrived at the village, the Chief told us, "As you know, there is Big Five. Do you know what is the Big Six? Maasai warriors!" Then, we watched the Maasai warriors do their high-jumping dance. Matt was invited to try out the dance since he was the only man in our group, then the chief said I could show them how to hula hoop. Several warriors attempted to hoop, and one was quite good at it. One warrior laughed so hard he actually fell down. I loved sharing my hoop with them.

Inside the village, we heard the women singing and the children hooped with me. We danced with the women, and by the end, everyone was smiling. I'd been learning Swahili but now I was learning Maasai, and my main word for the day was *supa*, which means "hello."

We were invited to visit a nearby school where the teacher wrote all the lessons on the blackboard with chalk and the children recited what was written in unison. I showed the students photos on my camera of the animals we'd seen on safari. I thought about my days of teaching and how every classroom was filled with books, manipulatives, and science experiments to encourage curiosity in every child. I was glad to be part of this philanthropy project helping fund the wish list to improve the school.

During our safari game drives, we saw the great migration of the wildebeest, hundreds of elephants, and many lions. When Duncan took us on our final game drive, we found the elusive black rhino. It was a dream come true to see all the Big Five during our adventures in Tanzania and Kenya.

46. KTLA TV Los Angeles travel segment
47. Tanzania: Country #100
48. Kenya: Country #101
49. African safari: Seeing the Big Five

Freefalling 50

As I approached my fiftieth new thing and my birthday, I knew I wanted to do something worthy and spectacular for my final challenge, as bold and brave as I could be. All along, people had been suggesting ideas for scary challenges. *What could it be?* Well, my entire life, I'd claimed I would never jump out of a perfectly well-maintained airplane. And now I was aware how far my limits had shifted over the year.

I thought about all the challenges I'd survived and how they'd built from the smallest thing (in some people's eyes), like tasting a new food, to the sheer horror of mountain biking—by far the scariest and hardest and full of overcoming past trauma. But I did it. I even enjoyed it after the crying. I now felt ready for something that would have seemed absolutely nuts to me in the past. I'd gotten to the point where I was brave enough to attempt this. My perspective was different.

I was invited to go to Oceanside near San Diego for the weekend to stay at a Thai-inspired hotel. It felt fitting to return to an Asian theme. I'd missed my time in Asia. I didn't feel ready to return to America when I left my marriage, but it was the choice I needed to make for my safety. I felt at peace with this choice for the start of my celebration. The PR team offered to set up my next challenge: GoJump Oceanside, the sky diving company. The idea terrified me. I'd never, ever wanted to try it before. But as I drove myself to the hotel, I contemplated how many of the fifty challenges were new or adventurous and how I'd succeeded with each one. Somehow, I kept saying yes. I never gave up. If I could call myself one year ago and explain everything that was going to happen, I would never have believed it and I probably would have hung up! I was already much more courageous than I ever imagined.

I sat on the balcony of my room, alone but not lonely. At every step, I'd always been nervous as well as excited. Every small hurdle I'd overcome had been leading up to this.

The next morning, I woke up and waited until it was time to drive to GoJump Oceanside. When I arrived, they told me that due to the cloud cover, I would have to wait. During the two hours, I talked with my trained tandem instructor. My guide asked me about my project. I mentioned a few things before getting to scuba diving with bull sharks. He said, "I would never do that. I'm afraid of sharks."

I was nearly unable to speak.

The man who flings himself regularly and for money as a job and changed his entire life to be able to train and continue to sky dive is afraid of sharks.

I am not so afraid of sharks.

He continued, "How can you be scared of sky diving if you scuba with sharks?"

For the first time, it hit me in a new way that "brave" is relative. I'd always thought of bravery as a light switch—one or the other. You either had it turned on and you were brave and did things, or you were in the dark and you weren't. As though being brave meant the same thing to all people. I realized "brave" is unique to each person. I wasn't afraid to scuba with sharks anymore because I was well-trained and had experience. This guy might have once been afraid to jump, but now he loved it. Not everyone was afraid of biking, but I had been, so it was brave for *me*.

My mind was blown.

If I let fear win and never tried, my life would be smaller, but I only needed to accomplish *my* tasks to push myself, not everyone else's. I wanted to grow and learn to approach new experiences with excitement instead of terror. It was one thing if something just wasn't for me, but I didn't want to be stuck. I didn't want to not jump out of a plane *only* because I was afraid to.

I told myself that I would say the *Shehecheyanu*, a Jewish blessing for the first time we encountered something new or arrived in a new place—or for me, a new state of being—in the plane. It wasn't the first time I thought to say this prayer as part of my 50 Things project. One of the reasons I wanted to leave Asia, and eventually Fred, was that I was missing my connection to community and Judaism. Prayers comfort me and I found the need to celebrate these new moments. My life was literally evolving as I watched. I'd stood on ships in Alaska when I was working and watched the glaciers calve. I could see the change happening with the refrigerator-sized pieces.

Now I was strapped to another human being with five points of connection, and as I trusted him to guide me with the parachute safely back to earth, I reflected on how much I had changed. It wasn't always obvious at every moment but having completed fifty tasks and reached my fiftieth birthday, I gained clarity. My perspective had shifted during the entire process of completing each challenge along the way.

When he pushed off the edge, we free fell away from the plane. I saw the ocean and the sky and the plane and the other people. We flew through the air like a bird. The wind pulled my face backward and the earth rushed up at me. And then we peacefully floated like clouds.

When I first left Fred, many people told me I was brave, and it was the opposite of what I felt about myself. In fact, I looked up the word in the dictionary several times trying to understand what was missing. Now, I knew I was brave. I was willing to try nearly anything. Fred was anything but brave. When he was angry, he pushed me to the ground from the back. Only a coward shoots you from behind where you cannot defend yourself. He treated me poorly many times and could have paralyzed me on our final day together. I stood up to his bad behavior and I never went back to him. During our separation and my divorce, I read countless books trying to find my way and understand how to cope with all the frustration, disappointment, and failure.

I changed paths from medicine to education and then to Club Med and cruise ships. I got divorced and I started again. I taught and traveled more and tried many ideas of how to live my life. Now after my fiftieth challenge, for my fiftieth birthday, it was time to celebrate. I jumped out of a plane and flew like a bird. I would be able to overcome whatever came next.

On Friday, the day after my birthday, for Shabbat, I chose to immerse myself in mikveh, a traditional time of purification and preparation for a change in role. I'd done this before my wedding as well. Both times, I based my ceremony on the seven wedding blessings and invited women to join me in community. My intention after my divorce was to be ready for the commitment to myself and for growth and healing. It was a time of transition and uncertainty. I changed my name, reclaimed myself, but it didn't negate my past. I was moving forward to a new chapter, but I only had to turn the page. This path had been my own journey from the narrow places in my life, and now, through the flowing living waters of the mikveh, I was ready to move fully forward.

> Choice is empowerment when we choose to live differently, to be better. With every choice we defy inertia, with every choice we expand our sense of possibility. With every choice we become emboldened. But it is not easy, nor is it linear. We go back and forth between choice and discernment, reaffirming our decisions, reexamining everything. The spiritual path is a zigzag, a switchback up a mountain. It is exhausting, riddled with doubt and setbacks. There are so many ways to get us where we need to go. —Rabbi Karyn Kedar, 30 Nisan, 15th day of Omer

> Excerpt from *Amen: Seeking Presence with Prayer, Poetry, and Mindfulness Practice*, by Rabbi Karyn Kedar © 2020 by Central Conference of American Rabbis. Used by permission of the CCAR. All rights reserved.

At first, I was discouraged, depressed, even (at times) suicidal, but now I could see that each tiny little thing had added up to a whole new part. In my mikveh ceremony after my divorce, I used prayers that were blessings for being Jewish, for being a woman, for the mikveh, and one I learned about in my studies which is the

Birkat ha-Gomel prayer which is a "traditional prayer of thanks to be recited by one who has survived a dangerous situation."

The prayer says:

> *Brukhah at yah eloheinu ruakh ha'olam, ha'gomelet l'khayavim tovot, sheg'malani kol tov.*
>
> Blessed are You, Adonai our God, ruler of the Universe, who bestows kindness on those who are committed, and who has granted to me all kindness.

Community response:

> *Mi she'g'malaikh kol tov, hee tigmalaikh kol tov, selah.*
>
> May the One who has granted you all kindness always grant kindness to you, selah.

When I first read this prayer, I learned it's one you say after having a near miss with something terrifying. It felt fitting to me to remember how scared I was and how much my world had broken along with my marriage. I had quit my job, sold my car, and rented out my condo to try to make my relationship work. And when it failed so spectacularly, I felt like I had to start from scratch, but that isn't how life works. There were lessons that helped with the next phase, and it was more like a spiral moving upward. There are times when you're lower than the top of the last spin, but then as you move up again, you climb higher than ever before. I remember crying at the magazine conference about not having the journalism-specific knowledge, but after some Googling, I started to understand the vocabulary much like I learned about MI and IPM on the ships. I had a different set of experiences that were valid and would help me on my journey. I had to remember all I had already accomplished.

I also said a blessing for forgiveness with a special thought to forgiving myself:

"Blessed are You, Source of Life, for granting us the power of forgiveness, of tshuva, and for inspiring us to turn toward the light of goodness and the power of peace. Blessed are You, Source of Life, for forgiving us and pardoning our wrongdoings, allowing us to begin again each day."

I thought about how hard it was to forgive myself and change my ideas about my relationship when my marriage ended, and another of Rabbi Karyn D. Kedar's writings spoke to me so much I included it in my ceremony:

> As we strive to love others, we often forget to love ourselves. It is as if self-love is forbidden. But actually it is commanded in the Bible. The command is not only to love our neighbor, but to love our neighbor as we love ourselves. As we deepen the love for ourselves, we deepen the capacity to love others. Love heals. It heals the wounded soul, it heals the relationships we cherish, it heals the world. Self-love strengthens our ability to be loving beings. —*Love Heals: Day 33 Omer, God Whispers*
>
> Excerpt from *God Whispers: Stories of the Soul, Lessons of the Heart* by Rabbi Karyn Kedar © 2000 by Jewish Lights Publishing. Used by permission of Rabbi Karyn Kedar. All rights reserved.

It was important to include the *Mi Shebeirach* version by Debbie Friedman, the blessing about healing and renewal for our loved ones, ourselves, and the world.:

Mi shebeirach avoteinu, M'kor hab'racha l'imoteinu
May the source of strength, Who blessed the ones before us.
Help us find the courage to make our lives a blessing.
And let us say Amen
Mi shebeirach imoteinu, M'kor habrachah l'avoteinu

Bless those in need of healing with r'fuah sh'leimah
The renewal of body, the renewal of spirit.
And let us say Amen.

I was introduced to the artist, Judy Chicago, by my teacher and friend, Joannie Parker. Joannie shared this meaningful poem with me, which we read at my ceremony:

Merger Poem
by Judy Chicago

And then all that has divided us will merge.
And then compassion will be wedded to power
And then softness will come to a world that is harsh and unkind.
And then both men and women will be gentle.
And then both women and men will be strong.
And then no person will be subject to another's will.
And then all will be rich and free and varied.
And then the greed of some will give way to the needs of many.
And then all will share equally in the earth's abundance.
And then all will care for the sick and the weak and the old.
And then all will nourish the young.
And then all will cherish life's creatures.
And then all will live in harmony with each other and the earth.
And then everywhere will be called Eden once again.

The final blessing I chose was to celebrate making it to this new time, and was one I'd been using lately in my challenges, the Shehecheyanu:

> *Baruch atah, Adonai Eloheinu, Melech haolam, she-hecheyanu, v'kiy'manu, v'higiyanu laz'man hazeh.*

> *Blessed are You, Adonai our God, Sovereign of all, who has kept us alive, sustained us, and brought us to this season.*

I chose to celebrate by myself, with my Jewish community, through study with my rabbis, at Shabbat Services, and at the mikveh near my house at American Jewish University.

On Saturday night, two days after my actual birthday, I had a huge party at my parents' house with more than a hundred friends. My college friends flew in from San Francisco and Philadelphia, my sister arrived from New York City, we had music and food, and people from all the disparate parts of my life met in real life. I felt blessed and beloved. I felt honored that people chose to spend my special day with me. Not so long ago, I feared there was something deeply wrong with me and I would never smile or laugh again. Now, I realized my life was full of magic again. Many people cared about me, supported me, and wanted the best for me. I was grateful for my good health and opportunities, because it wasn't that long ago that I was lying on the sidewalk, in shock, and in physical and emotional pain in a small city in northern Thailand.

But on this night, and moving forward, I knew how much love and respect I both deserved and could give. I put the nightmares away and danced all night long. Happy birthday to me!

50.   Skydiving—Happy 50th birthday to me!

Return to Vanuatu

One year later, I was back at the Travel Classics conference in Tucson when my latest KTLA segment aired. I realized that it was my third time at this conference. The first time, in Scottsdale, I cried in my hotel room and didn't know what "J-School" was but still sold three pieces. The second time was in Ireland/Scotland, and my KTLA producer emailed me while I was there that I was nominated for an award. Now at the third one, I was on TV back in LA while at the conference!

Maren, who runs the conference and has always been supportive of me, introduced me to one of the sponsors as "Lisa, who has her own TV series."

I laughed and said, "I hope so—someday!"

I was on my way to the United Nations General Assembly and the Gates Foundation Conference in New York City to represent *Ms.* magazine at the United Nations Women's Meeting. I couldn't believe how much had changed.

As I keep traveling to new places and have many more adventures, I often think about the quote from J.R.R. Tolkien: "Not all who wander are lost." So many times, I have literally felt lost, due to my eye issues or losing what I thought was my chosen path, but every single time, with support from my friends and family, I have found myself on firm footing once again, able to explore in new, and possibly better, ways.

I remember reading Jerri Nielsen's book, *Icebound*, about when she worked, lived, and survived cancer in Antarctica. She wrote: "What I have learned from [the early polar explorers'] lives is that they truly lived. More and more as I am here and see what life really is, I understand that it is not when or how you die, but how and if you truly were ever alive." I thought about how she overcame her circumstances and how I have moved past so many obstacles. There are hardships and challenges that everyone must rise above. As the Japanese proverb says, "Fall down seven, get up eight." Over the years, I've noticed how many times I've had to change and invent new paths, but perhaps, I realized, it isn't the number that matters, only the moving forward. When I was on campus at the University of Pennsylvania, I often passed the Class of 1893 Memorial Gate, where the arched ironwork spells out the class motto in Latin: *Inveniemus viam aut faciemus*, which translates to, "We will find a way or we shall make one." I've been creating my own map and my own path and it has not all been on a paved highway. Some parts of my life have felt filled with potholes, dirt roads, flat tires, and hardship, but then there are parts full of sunshine, fields of flowers, and picnics.

When I was invited to return to Fiji and Vanuatu as part of a press trip, it felt like I had come full circle. This time, there's no fighting in the Fiji airport with Fred. When I was standing in the exact spot at baggage claim where our fight happened, I could see how that trip and ultimately our marriage unraveled. While I did cry in my room the first night in Vanuatu after someone asked me about the time I was here before, I could see differently now. I learned about myself, my perspective changed, and I would not tolerate that behavior again.

This time, I scuba dive again to 130 feet on the SS *President Coolidge* and remember being here before. I loved it the first time, and it's even better on this trip. I'm staying at a luxury boutique hotel, drinking from fresh coconuts for breakfast with my toes in white sand. I have a dive buddy who is friendly and excited that we're both scuba diving, and the only drama is when a bee stings me and my foot swells up. No one yells at me or pouts or causes trouble. We visit a local village, where I bring my hula hoop and school supplies for the children.

For the first time, I fly to Tanna, the island Fred and I did not visit because he thought the flights were too expensive. We stay at the lovely White Grass Ocean Resort and scuba dive there as well. The highlight of the entire trip is our trip to Mount Yasur, where we walk on the edge of an active volcano. I'm mesmerized watching the lava from the edge. We're wearing hard hats and car-rying flashlights. This is clearly not a safe ride at a theme park, this is active adventure. I hear the volcano rumble, I feel it shake, I smell the smoke, and I see the lava spark! I'm thrilled to have been invited to Vanuatu for this opportunity. I worked hard, and no matter how many times Fred told me, "No one wants to work with you," I never gave up on myself...although I did have to give up our marriage and get rid of *him*.

One night, I see a cute guy at the bar in our small hotel. We don't talk, but I see him again at breakfast and invite him to join me. He introduces himself. His name is Fred—of course. And I laugh. It's funny. There have been hard times but there is also laughter and hope, and I know this journey I'm on is worth it.

ACKNOWLEDGMENTS

Dear Reader,

Thank you for spending this time with me and my story in these pages. I hope you overcome the obstacles in your path small step by small step. I would love to hear about the challenges you courageously tackle. You can find me at LisaNiver.com and across social media @LisaNiver. If you or someone you love is in an unsafe situation or struggling with issues, I hope you will seek help, ask questions and offer support. It is a sign of strength to ask for assistance. We all need each other.

This book has taken an entire village of support especially during the uncertainty of the COVID coaster. Those of you who have taken my phone calls full of tears, know about my affection for stickers or have received one of my handmade cards hold a special place in my heart and I would not have made it this far without you. Unfortunately, thanking you each individually is not possible in these pages, but I look forward to our next meal where I can share my gratitude in person. Thank you for your generosity of time, spirit, and love.

You would not be holding this book in your hands or hearing it without my amazing agent, Chip MacGregor, and my awesome publisher, Debby Englander, who both believed in my book from the beginning. Thank you to the Post Hill Press Team: Anthony Ziccardi, Michael L. Wilson, Ashlyn Inman, Heather King, Caitlyn Limbaugh, Aleah Taboclaon, Sara Stickney, Conroy Accord, Anika Claire, Kate Harris, Morgan Simpson, Golda Ouano, and Jonathan

Karp and his superb team at Simon and Schuster. Thank you to Dr. Alan Brodney and Constance Kaplan who allowed me to have the perspective for this path.

I am always reading multiple books and I appreciate all of the authors who encouraged me and whose work inspired me and who I have interviewed for my articles on *We Said Go Travel* and my podcast, *Make Your Own Map*. Writing is rewriting and it would never have happened without my talented developmental editor, Ann Campbell, as well as Holly Corbett, David Hochman, Tiffany Hawk, Rachel Ng, Robin Catalano, Kate MacGregor and Maia Homstad.

To each and every one of my students, my teachers, the parents who came to help in my classroom, the teams who made every conference I attended, the PR teams and destinations around the world that inspired and assisted with my challenges great and small, the workshops I have attended especially at UPOD and Los Angeles Press Club, my schools who taught me important lessons, my dance partners, dive buddies, swim and art friends, my temple and every worship service that lifted my spirit, the ship captains, sunshine girls and crew that I sailed the seas with, my traveling companions and all my friends and family members, thank you. Thank you to my editors and writing friends and everyone who believed in me even when I did not think I could take on one more challenge, try one more way to make my writing, videos or social media happen, or pack my bags one more time.

I have learned from all of you how to create my own path. I look forward to using the tools and tips you have shared and continuing our journey together.

B'shalom,
Lisa Niver
2023

ABOUT THE AUTHOR

Author Photo Credit: Judith Gigliotti

Lisa Niver is an award-winning travel expert who has explored 102 countries on six continents. This University of Pennsylvania graduate sailed across the seas for seven years with Princess Cruises, Royal Caribbean, and Renaissance Cruises and spent three years backpacking across Asia. Discover her articles in publications from *AARP: The Magazine* and *AAA Explorer* to *WIRED* and *Wharton Magazine*, as well as her site WeSaidGoTravel. On her global podcast, Make Your Own Map, Niver has interviewed Deepak Chopra, Olympic medalists, and numerous bestselling authors, and as a journalist has been invited to both the Oscars and the United Nations. For her print and digital stories as well as her television segments, she has been awarded three Southern California Journalism Awards and two National Arts and Entertainment Journalism Awards and been a finalist twenty-two times.

Named a #3 travel influencer for 2023, Niver talks travel on broadcast television at KTLA TV Los Angeles, her YouTube channel with over 2 million views, and in her memoir.